Parapsychology:
An Insider's View of ESP

Parapsychology:

An Insider's View
of ESP

J. Gaither Pratt

The Scarecrow Press, Inc.
Metuchen, N.J.   1977

This edition is reprinted by permission
from the 1966 E. P. Dutton & Co., Inc.,
edition, with a new Foreword.
Copyright © 1964, 1977 by J. Gaither Pratt
Manufactured in the United States of America

Library of Congress Cataloging in Publication Data
Pratt, Joseph Gaither, 1910-
    Parapsychology.
    Reprint of the 1966 ed. published by Dutton, New York.
    Bibliography: p.
    1. Psychical Research   I. Title.
[BF1031.P753 1977]   133.8   76-45437
ISBN 0-8108-0991-5

Grateful acknowledgment is made to the following for use of published material:

American Scientist—Quotation from the "Correspondence Column" by Dr. G. Evelyn Hutchinson, the *American Scientist*, Summer 1948 issue. Reprinted by permission of the author and publisher.

Bruce Humphries, Publisher—Excerpt from *Beyond Normal Recognition* by John F. Thomas. Reprinted by permission of the publisher.

Journal of Parapsychology—Excerpt by Professor Hornell Hart from the *Journal of Parapsychology*, September 1947 issue. Reprinted by permission of the publisher.

The Society for Psychical Research—Excerpts from *Proceedings of the Society for Psychical Research*, 1920-21 and Volume 34, 1924; excerpts from the *Journal of the Society for Psychical Research*, 1890 and 1927. Reprinted by permission of The Society for Psychical Research.

To Ruth

Foreword to the
Scarecrow Press Edition

Parapsychology: An Insider's View of ESP, written in 1963, presents a personalized survey of research in parapsychology and renders an accounting on progress in the field as of that date. The primary emphasis of the book is not on the past, the history of scientific investigations of psychic phenomena, but upon the future. It presents the coming areas of research within the framework of a developing and ongoing revolution in human thought, an endeavor to make basic discoveries regarding the nature of life and its place in the universe.

In one sense, this book is more timely today than it was thirteen years ago. At that time its central theme —that the findings of parapsychology indicate that mind exists in its own right and has its own powers, including those of interacting with matter—may have seemed to many to be overbold and premature. But the rapid developments that have occurred in the field since that time lend additional support to the interpretation of the research as the science of mind. Anyone wishing to learn about the more recent advances in parapsychology after reading the account given here of earlier work could perhaps start with my book written as a sequel to this one, *ESP Research Today* (Scarecrow Press, 1973). It contains many references to other publications and thus will guide the eager student to much of the vast literature that is available.

Perhaps a few final words are needed to avoid possible misunderstandings. There will be little disagreement over the idea that the claims of the parapsychologists are revolutionary. Even the skeptics and opponents acknowledge this fact. But opinions vary widely regarding how and why the field deserves this description. Especially among active parapsychologists one finds that interpretations differ, ranging from the view that parapsychology is only a frontier of physics to the one offered in this book, that this research bids well to establish that life embodies forces that are beyond those encompassed by the science of matter. Such differences of opinion only show that the parapsychological revolution is still unfinished. There is room for honest (and healthful) disagreement because we do not yet know enough about the nature of psychic phenomena— even of those that parapsychologists agree are firmly established. And we also agree that the primary business of the research at this stage is to press for answers to questions about the nature of the paranormal processes we are studying. Only as we extend our understanding of these events will the full dimensions and form of the parapsychological revolution become clear and be universally accepted.

J. G. Pratt

"High Fields"
Keswick, Virginia
September, 1976

Acknowledgments

The book itself is offered as a token of appreciation to those many friends and colleagues with whom for thirty years I have shared ideas as well as efforts. Whatever qualifications I may have for this venture in popular writing have been immeasurably broadened by these associations. Then, during the four months' period of intensive effort during which the book was actually written, I have found the roll of those to whom I am immediately indebted growing week by week. Each of the following will know full well in what respect I owe him or her my special thanks: Lee Barker, Cree Duke, Joanna Galdamez, Gwen Glass, Tom Greville, Portia Hamilton, Joe Marks, Lillian Marks, Gareth McCoy, Dorothy McKittrick, Gardner Murphy, Karlis Osis, Dorothy Pope, Bill Roll, and Kathryn Tebbel.

Contents

Parapsychology:
An Insider's View of ESP

The Benign Revolution

In 1936 I became a professional revolutionist. This book is about the revolution I joined.

Before you start looking for the beard or calling the FBI, consider the meaning of the words. Webster says: "Revolution: A total or radical change; as, a *revolution* in thought." And a bit farther on: "Revolutionist: One engaged in a revolution."

One tends to think of a revolution as an act of violence and bloodshed, a power struggle that results in the overthrow of the government when it is successful and in the execution of the revolutionists when the plot fails. But the truth is that the political upheavals that hit the headlines are only passing symptoms of larger changes spanning decades or even centuries of history. The disturbances that meet the eye or ear are like the lightning flash and the thunder—here only briefly, and recurring a number of times at unpredictable times and places. But the more basic reality which they symbolize is the storm, an encompassing force with a history of origin, growth, movement, and consummate power. To appreciate the true nature of the storm, one must look beyond the lightning flashes and the thunderclaps. Similarly we must see beyond the surface symptoms to appreciate the real moving force which a total change in thought represents.

Examining the matter in this way, we discover that the really important thing about a revolution is a basic advance in ideas. First and foremost, it is a new way of thinking about a particular aspect of the universe. This is true whether it reaches outward along the largest dimensions of infinite space or focuses inward upon the smallest particles inside the atom. Or it may deal with human affairs, a general category within which the recurrent political upheavals make up a special group. The really major changes, however, have not been concerned with such local affairs as whether this or that government should prevail.

And so this book is about a revolution of human thought. Our Western culture has passed through a number of great changes in ways of thinking since the Renaissance, others are in the process of taking place, and many more will undoubtedly come in the years and centuries ahead. The advance in thinking with which this book is concerned is still in the process of taking shape. Indeed, it is even still in a very early stage of development, though not too early to be recognized and to be appreciated for what it has already accomplished as well as for its far greater potentialities yet to be appreciated. This is the revolution of thinking embodied in the new branch of science, parapsychology. The definition of this field is quite simple: as physics is the science which deals with matter, so parapsychology is the science of mind. So simple to state, yet so far-reaching in its implications! It will be the main task of this book to present some highlights of past accomplishments in this field and the general scope and direction of present efforts—and to explore and explain the meaning of its findings.

As the account develops chapter by chapter, I hope that the full import of this definition of parapsychology will become clear. At this starting point, the definition itself, offered without elaboration or complication, is the cornerstone upon which the structure built up over the following pages will be erected.

Yes, I *am* serious about this subject, and this is a serious work. It will be factual and provocative, not a visionary view of an imaginary world dreamed up in an ivory tower. Most of the views expressed are not original. Before my mind's eye as I write are the examples of many great thinkers who have voiced their convictions regarding the revolutionary nature and importance of parapsychology since the field began its organized existence eighty years ago. Nor am I lacking in company among my contemporaries who are actively interested in the movement. Let me illustrate by citing a scholar who addressed himself specifically to the question of the place of parapsychology in relation to other major developments in Western science and culture.

The statement relevant to the topic before us was in a book review in the *Journal of Parapsychology* for Sep-

tember 1947, written by Professor Hornell Hart, then
a member of the Department of Sociology of Duke University. He wrote as follows:

> Since the middle ages, human thought in Western
> civilization has passed through eight basic revolu-
> tions, which may be characterized as follows:
>
> 1. From the conception of a universe around a flat
> earth, to the conception of a cosmos in which our
> spherical earth revolves around its sun in one of in-
> numerable galaxies;
>
> 2. From government by dictatorial hierarchies, to
> democratic government, aspiring to be founded on the
> will of the people;
>
> 3. From magical alchemy and rule-of-thumb crafts-
> manship, to experimental research in physics and
> chemistry, with scientific engineering, and the result-
> ing industrial revolution;
>
> 4. From superstition in medicine, farming, diet,
> and other biological fields, to scientific research via
> microscope, chemistry, and statistics, with resulting
> revolutionary improvements in public health;
>
> 5. From the dogma of sudden creation, to the
> theory of evolution;
>
> 6. From the dogma of the indivisible atom, to
> modern electronics and the resulting development of
> our electrical civilization;
>
> 7. From dogmatic pedagogy and propaganda, to
> mental tests and attitude scales, with resulting pur-
> poseful progress in education; and
>
> 8. From the Newtonian system of mechanics, to
> Einsteinian relativity, with its resulting release of
> atomic energy and the precipitation of the Atomic
> Age.

Dr. Hart's penetrating outline of the history of Western thought was given as the background for what he lists as the ninth basic revolution of human thought. It was with this recent scientific change, as reflected at that time in Dr. J. B. Rhine's book, *The Reach of the Mind*, that he was really concerned. Again, Dr. Hart's words speak best for themselves:

> This revolution consists in the scientific demonstration that man is fundamentally mind-centered rather than brain-centered. . . . If steam pressure, electricity, and chemistry have placed vast powers at man's command, what of a revolution which demonstrates by laboratory methods that mind can contact mind without the aid of its senses and regardless of time and space, and that mind can control matter without physical contacts? As Dr. Rhine keeps pointing out, these discovered powers are still rudimentary, just as early discoveries in the field of electricity were rudimentary. But now that they have been demonstrated, the methods of expanding our control over them begin to become clear. The revolution is under way.

Most students of parapsychology will agree that the field has made a good start, but they will agree further that it is only a start. Yet we are compelled, when we consider the situation, to emphasize what has already been accomplished. Even if we can anticipate that this will later, in the light of history, seem rudimentary and groping, the future developments toward which we are struggling are a part of the unknown territory beyond our present frontier of knowledge.

When will we be able to say that this new science of
mind has been successfully established? When the new
point of view and the facts supporting it have been accepted by the leaders of thought and, through them,
have become a part of our culture and of the accepted
body of knowledge. The task of educating people to the
acceptance of this great change will not be an easy one.
It requires work—hard work—and the talents of many
different students of parapsychology, each one taking up
the challenge in the way best suited to his own qualifications and personality. This book is an effort to help
in spreading information about the search for new
scientific knowledge about mind and its place in the universe.

Anyone presuming to offer himself as a spokesman for
this complex, specialized, pioneer science of mind
should first check his own credentials. There is no doubt
about the fact that this is a subject which fascinates people in general. In any country where freedom of thought
is guaranteed, all it takes is the courage—some would prefer to say the foolhardiness—to venture into this new and
little-explored area. It is not surprising, therefore, that
among the great number of books that deal with this
"twilight zone" of puzzling experiences and with the
complex topic of experimental laboratory research on
parapsychological (or psi) phenomena there are many
that should never have been written. The parapsychologists will have no difficulty separating the chaff from the
wheat, but what about the general reader?

To this question there is no easy answer. In due time,
of course, the problem will become less serious. As peo-

ple become better informed about psi, they will be better able to judge what is good reporting and what is bad. Meanwhile, those who are qualified in parapsychology must do what they can to guide the general reader so that he feels justified, if he so desires, in spending some of his precious hours on this subject.

But how is the reader to know that the writer of the present book is not the most audacious pretender of all? I have learned from talking to visitors in the Parapsychology Laboratory of Duke University that people usually want to know how one happened to come into this field. Therefore, some notes about myself may be offered here for those readers who want to know something about the background and qualifications of the pilot who has offered to guide them on this journey into a new realm of ideas.

I was born in 1910, the fourth child in a farm family in the Piedmont section of North Carolina. I had six younger brothers and sisters. Thus, counting themselves, my parents proudly ruled over a family of twelve. Ten children were only slightly above the average number of offspring per family in our part of the country during the first quarter of the century.

My earliest intellectual—or was it emotional?—memory is of a fixed ambition to become a Methodist minister. I cannot remember when this decision was made. In any case, it became such a strong commitment on my part that I announced, freely and repeatedly, in the family and around the community, what I was going to do when I grew up. The idea had completely possessed me by the time I entered the first grade, and it lent strong purpose to all my studies until I was through college.

Not until the first semester of graduate study in the Duke University School of Religion did I finally pause long enough in the pursuit of this goal to realize that my mind was not suited to a profession in which the *answers* to the great questions regarding man and his relation to the universe are largely taken on faith. At that stage I went through a difficult personal and social readjustment of my plans for a career. I faced up to the realization, which had been dawning upon me for several years, that my interest in people was more than simply a desire to "do good" here and now. Instead, the desire to know more about what man really is had been growing until it outweighed my other, lifelong commitment. In February 1932, I switched courses and entered the Duke Department of Psychology.

This change, made in the middle of the school year, left me without any means of support. One of my former teachers, Dr. Rhine, asked me one day—almost incidentally in a chance meeting, as I recall—if I would like to become his research assistant in the experimental work he was doing in the area of extrasensory perception (ESP). I was interested. At that time the chance to earn fifty cents an hour looked good. My "scientific" attitude was one of open-minded curiosity strongly flavored with skepticism. Dr. Rhine gave me the general assignment of testing my friends and acquaintances to see if any of them appeared to have outstanding ability as ESP subjects. Thus began for me a period of active, but avocational, work in parapsychology which lasted until that fateful day in 1936 when I decided to become a full-time parapsychologist.

My main job during that four-year period was, of course, the pursuit of graduate studies leading to the M.A. (1933) and Ph.D. (1936) degrees. My life as a graduate student was, in itself, a full-time business, covering required courses and preliminary examinations during the first years and the Ph.D. thesis research project (an investigation of the nature of learning in white rats) after that. Thus I was leading, intellectually, a double life: working through the grinding requirements for the higher degrees in the ordinary manner; and devoting such time as I could spare to research in parapsychology, the subject that increasingly was becoming for me the major scientific challenge.

After I had completed the residential requirements and the research for my thesis, I spent two years at Columbia University working with Dr. Gardner Murphy in ESP research. This came about in an interesting way: Dr. Rhine had published his first book, *Extrasensory Perception*, in 1934. Dr. Murphy saw it as being, possibly, a major breakthrough in the field in which he had been primarily interested since his youth. In the hope of transplanting the ESP research methods developed at Duke and—as described in the above book—applied there with such great success, Dr. Murphy asked if I could be loaned to him at Columbia for a period. My support would come from Dr. Murphy, who felt he would like to use the royalties from one of his books for this purpose.

The two years were only moderately successful in

terms of ESP results, but they served one purpose at least: they sustained and strengthened my interest in parapsychology.

The meeting at which I decided upon parapsychology as a profession took place during the second year in New York. Dr. Rhine, Dr. Murphy, and I were in Dr. Rhine's hotel room. I have completely forgotten the date, but the essential details are clearly etched in my memory. We were discussing plans for the establishment of what we hoped would become a permanent parapsychology laboratory at Duke. Would I be interested in coming back to Duke next fall as a full-time member of the research staff? I was asked not to answer right away but to consider first another career that was also open to me. This was a regular teaching position in the Duke University Department of Psychology, offered on the condition that I should give up research in parapsychology. The members of the department felt that one faculty member working in this field was enough. There is no stop-watch record of the time I took to decide, but I do not remember having any difficulty. I cast my life for parapsychology.

There have been many opportunities since that meeting when I could have reversed this decision. One time was when the dean of undergraduate studies at Duke called me in to discuss a new opening in the Psychology Department. The year was 1942, shortly after the attack on Pearl Harbor. I declined the dean's offer and went into war work with General Motors in Detroit. Another time was when I could have stayed in industrial production. A third time was at the end of the war. I had spent the last two years in the service as an officer in the Bureau of Naval Personnel. The government wished to continue our units and wanted us to stay; but I could not get back to Duke fast enough. Then, long past the time when anyone might have expected anything of the sort, the psychology professor who had supervised my Ph.D. research, Dr. D. K. Adams, said that he would recommend me for a teaching position in a Midwestern university in the field of animal behavior if I were interested in a change. After two days to think about the matter, I expressed appreciation and said no.

So much for the personal story: the background from which I got onto the psi trail and the times when I read signposts at crossroads along the way and decided to go straight ahead instead of taking a side turning. The rest of the professional story: the past quarter century of study, research, writing, editing, question-asking and -answering, attending conferences, consulting with co-workers and visitors at home and abroad, and all those other things that a full-time parapsychologist does with his time. These activities are best treated as only an incidental part of the vast amount of work by the many investigators who have written this most recent epoch in the history of the field.

There are, of course, as many variations on the theme of how people have been attracted to or repelled by parapsychology as there are people who have been involved with the field. Some of these cases exhibit such distinctive features as to be worthy of special notice at appropriate places in later chapters. These personal ref-

erences and anecdotes add flavor to this unique development in human thought.

Let us return to the main theme of the chapter: what
this book is about in terms of the meaning, scope, and
contents of the field itself. Earlier, I ventured to suggest
that parapsychology is the science of mind. Parapsychology began when scientists frankly faced up to the questions posed by experiences from everyday life suggesting
action at a distance without any sort of physical contact.
These are experiences which suggest that man may be
capable of gaining knowledge of distant or future events
when there is no conceivable physical energy reaching
any of his sense organs. If these things have any real
basis in fact, then something more than the operation
of the laws of physics seems to be involved. Psi phenomena are precisely those subjective events which do
not lend themselves to explanation, either rationally or
theoretically, in wholly physicalistic terms. Thus, they
are those events which most strongly suggest that something beyond the phenomena of physics exists in the
universe. This aspect of reality we can quite properly call
by an old and familiar term—mind.

As I write, I imagine hearing a reader exclaiming:
"But *mind!* What's new about that? Men have been
talking and writing about mind since history began, and
they have been knowing it through direct experience at
least since the first ape man stood on his two hind legs
to try to get a banana which was out of reach and then
stopped to ponder his predicament. Don't tell *me* the
psi revolution has discovered *mind!*" Excuse me for a
moment while I try to win over the questioner so that

we can have unanimous agreement on this really basic issue.

True, we all do have an awareness of some of our own subjective experiences—what we ordinarily call consciousness or *self*-awareness. But does this justify our saying that *mind* is known and accepted as a scientific concept? Unfortunately, no. It is obvious when we think of the matter that introspective knowledge of one's own experiences is not a reliable guide to the truth about human nature. If it were, there would be no need for psychology and psychiatry as academic fields of research and study. Everyone would by the power of his own insights know his own inner nature, and if a citizen of ancient Greece had dared to speak the words, "Know thyself," he would have been hailed as a comedian rather than a sage.

But if introspection cannot tell us the basic facts regarding the *workings* of mind, how can we expect it to tell us the truth about the *existence* of mind?

The question is not an idle one. The history of philosophy shows that there has been a continual battle, waxing and waning over thousands of pages of unending and seemingly unendable debate, over what place, *if any*, mind occupies in the universe. Perhaps "unendable" is too strong a word, because the battle over the past couple of centuries has certainly been going strongly in favor of those philosophers and scientists who would say that *mind has no place at all!* This is the position which has been variously identified as mechanism, materialism, physical monism, logical positivism, and the like. It has become in scientific circles virtually a world view, owing to the great success which has already been achieved in extending the laws of physics and chemistry into those branches of science which are concerned with the nature and functions of living organisms. So great has this success been that it is not surprising that many have already come to believe that it is now only a matter of time until purely *physical* explanations will be found for all of the mysteries of life.

The revolutionary findings of parapsychology are the facts which cannot be accommodated to any view of the universe which equates all existence with those things that are the proper concern of physics: mass and energy operating within a space-time frame of reference. The psi facts *require* that we recognize that there is an additional quality in the realm of experience, a quality which is so unexpected from the point of view of accepted physiological principles that it inevitably suggests the presence in man of something beyond the physical aspects of the universe. This unique attribute in living beings we can, as I have already suggested, simply designate as *mind*.

This book, then, is the story of how a few scientists and scholars have proceeded over the past eighty years to investigate objectively and experimentally the most unusual, the most challenging claims in the realm of human experience. The investigations were aimed, in the first place, at finding out which, if any, of the claims that could not be reconciled with a mindless view of man could unmistakably be said to be grounded in *fact*. This phase of the psi revolution has already succeeded. Parapsychology has already produced findings that eventually must profoundly change the present scientific views of man and of his place in the universe. It will be the task of the remaining chapters of this book to give substance and force to this bald statement by outlining the developments that have already taken place in this new science of mind, not only in the Western world which gave birth to the movement and nurtured it through the difficult early years, but also as reflected by its expansion around the world.

To the extent that this presentation succeeds as an exercise in communication, the reader should, as he proceeds, have a growing appreciation of the fact that the subject matter of this book is something that profoundly affects *himself*, as it profoundly affects all men of this and future generations. We are even now moving toward a scientific reorientation of thought which no one can escape. Nor should anyone wish to do so, for this is an advance which bids well to place man as a person in a new and more proper perspective in the changing picture of his world that is being built up through science.

Already, parapsychology must give up the claim to being the latest radical development in thought. This distinction has been taken away from it most conspicuously by the exploration of space. But in the comparison of the psi and space revolutions we have a valuable lesson setting forth the fact that some great changes are favored by circumstances while others are accomplished slowly against heavy odds. Commenting upon the importance of the efforts to get an American to the moon, Mr. Walter Lippmann said: "It is one of the melancholy facts of political life that the good is not often sought for goodness' sake. Men are not easily moved to serve so great a purpose as the revolutionary increase of knowledge. So, we have to be prodded by the fear of being second and lured by the desire to be first." But what are we going to use as a stick and a carrot to get us to make a maximum effort in the most important of all searches for knowledge—the exploration of Man the Explorer?

Man needs to know himself, to know his own place in the order of things with the same calm assurance with which he knows that the earth revolves around the sun and that particular microbes cause particular diseases.

If there are phenomena in the world of experience that do not fit into our present scientific views of man, they may be the keys that will open the doors to new discoveries about human nature. Already it is possible to say with confidence that the question-raising, puzzling experiences from everyday life have led to actual experiments that have yielded supporting data from the laboratory. What some of these psi phenomena are and how far they advance us toward the new insights about mind we are seeking make up the topics of the chapters that follow.

Can anyone knowingly be indifferent toward studies of unusual effects in the realm of experience that offer as much promise of expanding our knowledge of human personality as we can now, by hindsight, see that the early studies of electrical sparks ultimately expanded our knowledge of the physical world? The question, it seems to me, is merely rhetorical, for the only answer that makes any sense is: No, certainly *not*. For those who agree, it is worth while reading on.

2

Puzzling Experiences

Parapsychology is one advance in thought which has a fairly clear historical origin. Its beginnings as an organized effort can be traced, and it is even possible to point to a specific occasion as the time when the basic new idea first began to take shape. One of the pioneers in the movement described an event which may well be credited with being parapsychology's historic starting point. But before we come to that occasion, it is necessary to say something about why—and how—anyone was able to appreciate the need for the radical change in scientific thinking that the developments that followed from that event are in the process of bringing about.

The nineteenth century sired several scientific revolutions. Consider the nine great upheavals in thought mentioned in Chapter 1. A surprisingly large number of them date from the 1800s. This is especially true for the great advances of science into the realm of living things: medicine, botany, zoology, and psychology. The nineteenth century was a period in which the earlier great triumphs over the mysteries of the physical universe seemed to most of the pioneers in the life sciences to provide the key to all of their puzzles as well. They were struggling to close the last remaining gap in a circle of knowledge which would, if successfully completed, bring the entire universe within one explanatory framework, the philosophy of materialism. The gap that had to be closed was that represented by life, and in its very center was man himself.

The revolution which appeared to many finally to have finished the job was the Darwinian theory of evolution. Here, it seemed, was the answer to the final great puzzle of how life itself, represented by the myriads of kinds of living things, had developed in a universe consisting totally of matter. The answer given was that it happened sheerly by accident! Life as we know it, Darwin said, has evolved by innumerable accidents following one upon another over the millions of years since an accidental joining of certain molecules in the waters of a cooling earth produced the first faint stirrings of life. Darwin's revolutionary contribution to thought was the bold suggestion that all subsequent forms of life followed from that first life-giving accident because of two circumstances. First, every living thing has the basic characteristic of attempting to stay alive, and it struggles against threats from its physical environment and also fights with other living things for the right to survive. Second, accidental changes continue to take place in succeeding generations of living organisms, and through these some forms become more fit for the struggle to survive and others become less fit. In the never ending fight for life the more efficient forms win out. So evolution advanced, worthy individuals clambering blindly and relentlessly upward over the carcasses of the weakling organisms that did not deserve to live—until man appeared, the crowning glorious accident!

See how beautifully simple and complete the picture is! The starting point a totally material earth . . . the first accidental life in some storm-stirred primordial ooze . . . the struggle to stay alive and the survival of the fittest . . . further accidents giving rise to different forms of life . . . the happy accident of sex and the power of reproduction enabling the survivors to produce further generations of the fittest fighters—with never a point in the whole process of evolution for any meaningful direction or purpose to enter upon the fatalistic stage. Where in this scheme of things is there room for mind?

Darwin himself, of course, had gone to nature during his famous voyage on the *Beagle*, the scientific expedition on which he observed the panorama of life in some of its most intense and undisturbed forms. It was out of his rich observations of nature's clues that he fashioned his theory. Indeed, the *fact* of evolution cannot be questioned. But any *theory* which says that the whole process has been nothing but a meaningless mutiny of molecules in a universe of matter is, as yet, only a theory.

I do not suggest that Darwin and other great materialists of like mind have not observed well. But have they observed widely enough? May nature herself not exhibit phenomena that cannot be explained in terms of physical mass and energy? Darwin was primarily a student of the behavioral or surface appearances of living things, and that may not be the best source of clues to the existence of mind.

Must we reconcile ourselves to being a part of this fantastic puppet show in which the pushes and pulls of atoms in random motion take the place of the puppeteer's strings? Or may we turn our attention once more to nature to see if there are essential parts of the picture that have been left outside the explanatory circle by which Darwin attempted to enclose all existence?

We must look for the traces of mind in the world of experience. And we must look especially at forms of experience which are unambiguous in the sense that they could not, if correctly reported, be explained in purely physical terms. *Are there any kinds of experience which defy explanation in purely physical terms and which therefore show that mind has its own place in the universe?*

In raising this question, we are not, of course, expecting final answers from what we may find in the way of personal claims and anecdotal stories. Rather, we want to know if nature offers us enough encouragement to look further. We are interested in the most *unusual things that people experience* because they tell us what kinds of questions we are justified in raising and how to set about seeking the answers through research.

The following accounts of experiences from everyday life, then, are intended to raise questions, nothing more and nothing less. As psi cases, they are *timeless* in the sense that they are typical of the ones that have been recorded throughout history. For this reason I have cited cases without regard to whether their dates of occurrence coincided with the historical era discussed later in this chapter. Even though the cases given here are recent, they are typical of those that were available to the founding fathers of parapsychology and which raised the same kinds of questions in their minds as the following accounts raise in ours. By giving attention to current cases we not only have the advantage of using fresh material but we also gain assurance that these experiences belong to our own day and time as much as to the culture of eighty or a hundred years ago. The use of this material is comparable to finding our own revealing formations in the surface of the earth to learn about geology instead of taking examples out of the first scientific treatises on the subject.

While I was working on this book at home, the phone rang. A lady, sounding excited and distraught, asked if she could talk to me for a while. When I asked who she was, she said that she would prefer to talk without giving her name. I told her to go right ahead.

She then described an incident which had happened in her home just two days before. She said that her family has two house keys which are different in appearance, one for the front door and the other for the kitchen. When they are home both keys stay at a certain place on the living-room mantelpiece.

When she returned to the house with her husband two days before, he placed the kitchen door key on the mantel in its usual place beside the other one. She had seen him do this, and both of them remembered seeing that both keys were there. The next day her husband asked where the kitchen door key was. Neither one of them had used it. They both searched for it without success.

Later their son came in, and they asked him about it. He knew nothing of it, and he also searched without success. The husband said that this was one time when it would be silly to make another key, since this one was bound to be right in the house. They simply had to find it!

She said that when both the husband and the son had gone to bed that night, she looked once more on the mantelpiece. The second key was simply not there! She decided to write some letters in the living room to allow time for her husband and son to get to sleep, then she intended to search again. After she had finished writing, she went once more to the fireplace to start her search in that area; and there was the key beside the other one, right where it belonged!

"Is it possible," she asked, "that I had the key all the time and that my subconscious mind had slipped it back there without my knowing it?"

"Of course that is conceivable," I said, "as shown by the fact that you have thought of that explanation yourself."

"But could it mean something supernatural? I don't think I *could* have put it there, but I just don't believe in the supernatural and I am afraid to think of anything like that as possibly being involved."

"No, it could not be the *super*natural, because there is no such thing. There is only the natural which we now know and understand, and there is the natural which is still beyond our present knowledge. Much of what people would have called the supernatural a few centuries ago we now accept and apply in our daily lives; and what we sometimes think of today as the supernatural our descendants will know about and use to their own benefit as something entirely natural. If the return of the key was not an act carried out in a momentary state of loss of memory on your part, this does not mean that some supernatural agency invaded your home to play tricks on you.

"In the Parapsychology Laboratory at Duke we have for years been doing experiments to test the old adage of 'mind over matter.' We have had subjects concentrate upon falling dice to see if they could make them turn up according to their wishing. Sometimes they have tried to get a larger-than-chance number of one face, then of another face, until they have wished for a high score on each face of the same dice for the same number of trials. In this way we are certain that the good results cannot be due to any physical bias in the dice themselves. Our results from many experiments have given such high odds against the interpretation that only lucky chance coincidence was involved that any open-minded person who looks at the evidence should agree that the *subjects were producing evidence of mind over matter*.

"Sometimes, also, there happen instances of unexplained physical occurrences in everyday life. While these do not by themselves prove that what we call, in our scientific language, psychokinesis (or PK) really occurred in each instance, the results of the laboratory PK experiments do justify our keeping our minds open to this possibility. And so, while I do not accept this explanation, neither would I want to dismiss outright the idea that your wanting that key so badly had, in some way we cannot yet explain, something to do with its coming back without your actually placing it there."

I then went on to mention that parapsychologists had for many years been actively interested in the collection and study of such unexplained physical happenings. We had, for example, made a close study of a house on Long Island in 1958 where dozens of unexplained physical disturbances took place (see Chapter 5).

My caller then said that she had *many* strange experiences, some of which seemed to predict the future, and they almost always came true. Would I be interested to hear about some of them? Yes, I said, of course. Thus encouraged, she went on to relate the following personal experiences.

The speaker—let us call her Mrs. X—said that she works in a factory in Durham. Some time ago, when she was at the drinking fountain, she saw a "vision" (in more technical language, a hallucination) of the son of the lady who worked next to her. The boy was lying dead on the ground in a strange position as the result of an accident, and there was blood all over him and on the ground. When Mrs. X went back to her work she told her neighbor that she should be prepared for some bad news about her son. It would come before she went home at the end of the day. The news arrived. The accident had happened just as Mrs. X had foreseen.

Another time she told a fellow worker at the plant that she ought to go home on the coming weekend to visit her father since he was going to die the next week from a heart attack. He did.

Again, Mrs. X said that she was in the car going with her family to visit relatives who lived out of town. She suddenly had an impression (not a vision) that a daughter in the family they were going to visit had fallen and received a bad cut over one eye. The moment the car drove in the yard the mother came out to greet them and told them that the little girl had fallen and suffered a bad cut over one eye just a short while before.

Finally, Mrs. X told about something that had happened before she moved to Durham. A small boy in the neighborhood had been lost. After a time his two shoes were found inside a pig lot on a nearby farm. An extensive search failed to discover any further trace of the boy, and the idea was offered that he had been eaten by the pigs. After a time this explanation of his disappearance was accepted. It bothered the lady who owned the farm so much that she came to Mrs. X and asked her to use her psychic powers to try to get some information about what had happened. Mrs. X told me that she could not say a thing, that these things simply did not happen to her that way. But it was on her mind while she went about her business. After some time she suddenly saw the body of the boy in a particular place. She told the lady where they should look, and that was where the boy was found—dead.

Our long conversation was drawing to a close. I explained that we have been collecting experiences such as hers, and Dr. Louisa E. Rhine has now built up a collection of more than 10,000 such experiences. She had been studying them for several years and publishing scientific articles about them. Just recently she wrote a popular book summarizing her findings. This book, I told Mrs. X, would be a good place to start if she would like to read about how these things happen to other people—to millions of people, we now can say with assurance.

Mrs. X wanted to get Dr. Rhine's book, and I told her that the name of it is *Hidden Channels of the Mind*. I invited her to call me up again and said that I did not mind if she wanted to wait until then to give me her name. Meanwhile, would she object if I wrote down what she had already told me for possible use in my book? She agreed, and I sat down immediately to type out the above account.

Another case involved a woman living in my home town (Winston-Salem, North Carolina), who wrote to the Parapsychology Laboratory shortly after World War II to relate the following experience shared between herself and her soldier son, who was stationed on the Mexican border. One night she dreamed that her son was about to be attacked by a bandit while he was asleep. She awoke to the sound of her own voice screaming his name. A few days later she got a letter from him saying that she had saved him from a bad spot. He had been on guard duty at night and had fallen asleep. He heard her calling him and woke up just in time. A moment after he heard her voice the officer in charge came by to check his post.

Recently a correspondent wrote that when he was living in Poland before the war he had known the engineer Stephan Ossowiecki, who gained a world-wide reputation for his ability to use ESP to help people in times of crisis by giving them facts that he could not have known in any ordinary way. He always tried, when asked, to give information that was needed about lost loved ones or valuable possessions. Our correspondent told of one such experience which happened in connection with an international balloon race staged in Poland in 1936. The two-man team of each country competing in the race went aloft in its balloon, and the winner was to be the team that touched ground at the greatest distance from the starting point. Within a few days all of the balloons had been reported except that of the Polish team. When several days of waiting and searching brought no news, those in charge turned to Mr. Ossowiecki for help. He worked over a map showing the part of Europe to the northeast from Poland, the direction in which the balloons had been carried by the winds. In a short time he put his finger down on a small island in the White Sea north of Russia and said that he saw two men there. They were suffering from exposure and hunger and the rescue should be made as quickly as possible. Then, in excitement, he said that they were about to be attacked by a polar bear, but that they remained quiet and the bear went away. The Polish authorities got in touch with the government of the U.S.S.R. and requested that a search plane be sent to that island. The plane went out, picked up the two lost balloonists, and brought them back.

When the men were questioned, they said that they were not in any great danger except for the time when they thought they might be attacked by a bear.

A book on parapsychology published in 1962 in Russia by Professor L. L. Vasiliev recounts a number of spontaneous psi experiences from his own country. In one of these cases, a wife of a soldier dreamed that she received a telegram from her husband telling her to meet him in a distant city. This was not the place where she knew he was stationed, but another town where their daughter was living at the time. No telegram was received, since none was sent. But the "message" was so vivid and clear that the wife requested the necessary time off and permission to travel in order to make the journey. Shortly after she arrived at the daughter's place there was a knock at the door. When the daughter answered it, she found her father, who spoke first and asked if her mother had come. The soldier was being sent to the front and he had a two-hour stop in that city. He had thought of wiring his wife to come to see him there but had decided against doing so.

A man in California wrote to the Parapsychology Laboratory as follows: "My wife died February 4. The second night after her death I felt her presence so strongly I said, 'If you are here and can hear me, give me a sign.' In a moment, a metal chariot, two horses made of metal akin to lead, perched atop the chime clock on the mantel *came tumbling down with a crash!!* It had been in that same place for twenty years and had never fallen."

Another case involving a physical effect that seemed to have a psi connection was received from a woman in Indiana. She wrote: "The night my sister died, her picture, in another sister's home eight miles away, fell from the wall. The glass was shattered; although it seemed impossible, the photograph was wedged between the wall and the baseboard."

In the same general class is this case reported by a man in Ohio: "One Sunday afternoon I was sitting at my desk reading. Suddenly, I felt a surge of blood racing through my veins; and at the same time a picture of a close friend hanging on the wall above my desk dashed to the floor, breaking the glass but not injuring the photograph. Even before picking up the picture I sat down to the typewriter and wrote to the friend concerned. He lived about 700 miles away. In due time I received a reply giving the address of a hospital. It seems that at the precise instant the picture fell and I felt the sudden increase in blood pressure my friend was driving his car across a railroad track and was struck by the locomotive."

We all know, of course, of the grandfather's clock, immortalized in song, that "stopped—short—never to go again when the Old Man died!" Next to the unaccountable falling of pictures and other objects, cases of clocks or watches stopping at the moment of death or a crisis are the most frequent. One correspondent related: "After my father died, which was 6:20 P.M., my kitchen clock (which had been his) stopped working at 6:20 every night for two weeks. And as for the clock, which is ticking away in my kitchen right now, it's about one hundred and twenty-five years old. . . . The clock was in the kitchen at the time of his death, but his bedroom was close by on the ground floor. The reason he was so conscious of the time, all the time during his lifetime, was that he was a railroad engineer. Almost to his last breath he'd keep asking us, 'What time is it?'"

(I had finished typing the preceding paragraph in one corner of our family kitchen while my wife, twenty feet away, was preparing Sunday breakfast. Suddenly she started to whistle the tune, "My Grandfather's Clock." I do not think I had given any outward sign of thinking about the song, and my wife said she couldn't explain what brought it to her mind.)

More than once over the years in the Parapsychology Laboratory I have heard Dr. Rhine refer to the strange thing that happened to him and his wife shortly after they came to Duke in 1927. Dr. Rhine was acting as a consultant to Mr. (later Dr.) John F. Thomas of Detroit, Michigan, for his research on the question of mediumship. Mr. Thomas was seeking a Ph.D. in psychology at Duke University under Professor Mc-Dougall on the basis of this study. Dr. and Mrs. Rhine were returning to their apartment after a conference at Duke in which Mr. Thomas' work was discussed. When they unlocked their apartment door and entered the living room a book was lying in the middle of the floor. There was a space on the bookshelf where it had been.

There was no evidence that anyone had been in the apartment during their absence. The title of the book on the floor was *Evidence of Things Not Seen.*

Dr. Louisa Rhine observed that her daughter Betsy, the third child in the family, frequently said things that suggested a telepathic bond between them. Mrs. Rhine began keeping a personal journal of the times when Betsy said something "out of the blue" that Mrs. Rhine was thinking about. Betsy was the only one of her four children who showed these spontaneous ESP occurrences in daily life frequently enough to justify keeping a special record of them. The events in which Betsy featured stirred Mrs. Rhine's interest in ESP in children. She carried through in her home a series of tests with ESP cards in which her own children and their friends in the neighborhood were used as subjects. In these, Betsy (then age three) scored impressively above the chance level, but she did not do as well as her older brother and sister.

It seems to me that my own life has been particularly barren of spontaneous psi experiences. Nor do I remember that these things were mentioned often in my family when I was growing up. I do remember one incident in my own experience that was connected with a search for an Indian arrowhead in a rocky field on our family farm. This was a field in which we had found an arrowhead previously, and I very much wanted to find my own. When my search failed, it occurred to me that if I picked up a stone and threw it some distance away I would find an arrowhead where it landed. I threw the stone, went to where it lay, and there beside it was my arrowhead!

What can one say about such experiences? The answer to this question will be one of the main concerns of this book. The matter is too complicated to explain fully in a few words. But some things we may perhaps agree upon right off.

One is that we should not simply deny that such experiences occur or ignore them. They *do*, rather more often than we ordinarily realize to be the case. So we can move on to the issue of what importance we should attach to them.

Should we say that they happen relatively infrequently, and then only very briefly and unpredictably; and that therefore we can dismiss them as of no importance? If so, shall we also dismiss comets and earthquakes, which are also relatively rare and of relatively brief duration?

Should we say that those that are not merely chance coincidences are probably largely the result of overwrought imaginations, exaggeration, or even outright fabrication? No, we shouldn't, for the simple reason that this is to *classify* the experiences on a basis of which we cannot be sure and in a way that would minimize their importance.

Shall we then conclude that they *are* what they appear to be, which would make them of maximum importance: proof of the powers of mind to operate without restrictions of space, time, and mass? Again, not at all!

The reports are still only anecdotal cases, and science rarely reaches final conclusions by relying entirely upon anecdotes.

But if none of these attitudes toward psychic experiences from everyday experience is acceptable, what can we think about them? Is there anything left?

Yes, we can ponder them.

We can see what questions they raise regarding, first, the different ways in which mind may interact directly with the outside world—that is, without the use of the senses and without the aid of the muscles or through any special instrumentation. When we examine them from this point of view, we discover that the kinds of experiences all fall under two general headings: extra-sensory perception (ESP) or psychokinesis (PK). ESP is the act of becoming aware of, or otherwise responding to, an external object, event, or situation which is beyond the reach of the sense organs. PK is the act of exerting an influence upon an outside physical object, event, or situation without the direct use of the muscles or any physical energy or instruments.

Further study of the wide range of psi experiences that occur under natural conditions reveals that three kinds or modes of ESP are distinguishable on the basis of the relation between the experiencing *subject* and the nature or condition of the experienced object or *target*. Telepathy is the ESP of another person's thought or purely subjective state. Clairvoyance is the ESP of a physical object, event, or situation that is not known to any person at the time. Precognition is the ESP of a future event that is beyond the reach of logical inference and that is not in any way later influenced or produced to make the target fit the prediction.

Extracting the essential terms from the foregoing two paragraphs suggests that the main outline of the field of parapsychology might be reduced to six words:

> Extrasensory perception
> Telepathy
> Clairvoyance
> Precognition
> Psychokinesis

This list is not intended to set fixed boundaries for the field, and it will be interesting, as we proceed, to see if we encounter any psi phenomena which make it necessary to extend this outline.

It is time now to take up once more the thread of events which marked the beginning of organized scientific interest in psi phenomena and to scan briefly the developments of the first fifty years. In the present chapter we shall be particularly interested in those early efforts which laid the groundwork for the field as a branch of laboratory, experimental research. In Chapter 7 ("Does Mind Survive Death?") we will be dealing with another topic which was a major area of emphasis for the workers of the early years.

What, then, was that special occasion which marked the birth of the psi revolution? It was identified by F. W. H. Myers, then already well known as a classical scholar, with a walk which he took in 1869 with Henry Sidgwick, professor of philosophy at Cambridge University. Myers relates that he asked Sidgwick if he thought there might be any way in which the basic questions about the nature of man and his place in the universe—questions that tradition, intuition, and metaphysics had not adequately solved—might be answered by the methods of objective scientific study. He says that Sidgwick answered that he had long been interested in the possibility of dealing with these questions by empirical methods through research. Largely out of the ideas born on this moonlight walk in Cambridge there emerged, in 1882, the Society for Psychical Research (S.P.R.).

This organization counted among its founders some of the leading British scholars of that time. And it has continued, during its uninterrupted history of more than eighty years, to attract to its membership and to its positions of leadership some of the truly great minds of our era. Among those who have belonged to the S.P.R. have been not only Henry Sidgwick, its first president, and F. W. H. Myers, but Sir William Barrett, Sir Oliver Lodge, Sir William Crookes, Charles Richet, F. C. S. Schiller, William James, Gilbert Murray, William McDougall, C. D. Broad, H. H. Price, R. H. Thouless, and Gardner Murphy. All of the above have served as president of the society.

There sprang up in America two years after the founding of the S.P.R. the American Society for Psychical Research. This has not enjoyed an uninterrupted history or reached the same lustrous level in its membership as the British society; but it has been effective nevertheless, and especially over the past twenty-five years it has pursued a serious program of study and research directed from its headquarters in New York.

I should mention in passing, also, that other countries have had their societies for research on psi, the collective, general term by which present-day parapsychologists designate the wide range of challenging phenomena with which they are concerned. Holland, France, the Scandinavian countries, Italy, Greece, and Czechoslovakia have had societies dating back many years and, more recently, such organizations have been formed in Argentina, South Africa, and Japan. Not all of these have done work that is within the areas of research with which this book is concerned. All of them must, as a matter of convenience, be left with only this brief mention.

While the founders of the S.P.R. were sure about their objectives, they were not equally clear about the definition of their field. They took as their domain the investigation of claims and observations of phenomena that, if found to have any basis in fact, would challenge explanation in terms of recognized physical laws. But they were not sure as to just what problems should be admitted under this general working definition. Thus, in addition to the effects that clearly would come under the headings of ESP and PK, they also had, at the start, a committee for the investigation of hypnotism. As time passed and the S.P.R. became better launched on its program, the investigators gradually got rid of the excess baggage of borderline problems that did not really belong within the field of parapsychology.

One of the first major tasks undertaken was to conduct a large-scale survey of ESP experiences from everyday life. Answers to a questionnaire were obtained from 17,000 people, of whom 1684 or nearly ten per cent said that they had had at least one spontaneous parapsychical experience that was convincing to themselves. The investigators then followed up as many of these cases as possible in order to verify the facts.

The investigators attempted to make an objective evaluation in the hope of converting this material into crucial evidence for the occurrence of telepathy—a very difficult task! We can now see that it was well-nigh hopeless as far as convincing a skeptical scientific world was concerned. (This idea of attempting to present case material as conclusive evidence is not, as we shall see, one that is very much used in parapsychology today.) But the study was productive and successful in a number of other ways. It provided material that was convincing to many of the research workers and thus it encouraged them to feel that they were on the right track. Most of all, it provided a rich store of information about the wide range of conditions under which ESP enters into daily life. The collection and study of cases became a major and permanent concern of parapsychologists.

But the quickest and greatest returns came from experiments in telepathy. In fact, the investigators were themselves surprised at how much evidence for telepathy apparently could be had for the asking. Within the short span of two years experiments were done with selected high-scoring subjects who produced results that were beyond the reasonable range of lucky coincidences. These involved the guessing of such things as lotto numbers, playing cards, and other common objects. Maintaining the highest standards of self-criticism, the members of the investigating committees were nevertheless convinced that the results provided conclusive evidence for ESP. Since they strongly leaned toward the telepathic explanation, they did not hesitate to so interpret their results in spite of the fact that the "sender" in the tests almost always looked at the physical object upon which he was concentrating his thoughts. The subject could use his ESP to identify either the sender's thought (telepathy) or the physical object itself (clairvoyance), but the latter was dismissed as a less reasonable possibility.

By 1885 the research workers had published several reports supporting their conclusions that telepathy occurs. Between that time and 1910 more than fifty additional experimental studies were conducted and reported, most of them with significant results.

Not all of the experiments were done with target material which lent itself easily to mathematical evaluation. There were some non-quantitative experiments in which the sender looked at a drawing of an object selected at random and the subject attempted to reproduce the picture without having any hint of what it might be. In some instances the results were so successful that the fact was obvious without statistics. Indeed, some scientists, like some laymen, do not feel fully at home with statistical analysis, and they are more easily convinced by the results of such "qualitative" tests. A few years ago Sir Alister Hardy, professor of zoology at Oxford University, gave some encouragement to the parapsychologists when he revealed that he was among

the number who had been won over to our cause. He
delivered a major address before a gathering of British
scientists in which he said that he had been convinced
of the reality of telepathy since his youth when he read
the reports of the early tests made with drawings. (He
had, however, considered it prudent to wait until he was
nearing the end of his scientific career before publicly
announcing his acceptance of telepathy. When he finally
did so it was in an address in which he offered suggestions regarding the possible role of telepathy in evolution.)

When I heard Sir Alister speak at the Ciba Foundation Symposium on ESP in London in 1955, he still
retained his preference for qualitative tests in which the
subject is given a freedom of choice comparable to that
found in the situations from everyday life in which ESP
occurs spontaneously.

An interesting series of demonstrations of telepathy
were those that Gilbert Murray, a member of the faculty
at Oxford, gave during the early years of this century.
Professor Murray discovered that he had a remarkable
ability to receive parapsychically the details of some complicated theme or scene, such as one selected from literature. He would go out of the room in his home where
members of his family and/or a few close friends were
gathered, being careful that he was out of earshot. Someone in the group who was going to act as the agent
(sender) would then decide what the target should be.
He spoke it softly, and it was written down for the
record. Then Professor Murray was called back into the
room. Generally, while trying to receive the correct im-

pressions, he held the hand of the sender. In view of the complexity of the themes chosen and the accuracy of many of Professor Murray's answers, it is difficult to see how this degree of contact could have provided any real help in the form of sensory cues.

Among the agents were Professor Murray's daughter and her husband, the historian Arnold Toynbee. The following are three tests which Professor Murray took while they were present.

Theme. Mrs. Arnold Toynbee (agent): "I think of the beginning of a [story by] Dostoievesky where the dog of a poor old man [is] dying in a restaurant."

Result. Professor Murray: "I think it's a thing in a book. I should think a Russian book. A very miserable old man, and I think he's doing something with a dead dog. [A] very unhappy one. I think it is in a restaurant and people are mocking, and then they are sorry and want to be kind. I am not sure." ("Nationality?") "No—I don't get their nationality. I have a feeling it is a sort of Gorki thing. I have a feeling that it is something Russian." [Note: Professor Murray had not read the book.]

Theme. Mrs. Arnold Toynbee (agent): "This is the girl in *The Cherry Orchard*, by Tchekoff, saying— 'When I was in Paris I went up in a balloon.'"

Result. Professor Murray: "I think this is a Russian story—a particular sentence, words 'De dum dum de dum dum—I went up in a balloon.' 'When I was the something, I went up in a balloon'—'when I was in Paris, I went up in a balloon.'"

Theme. Mr. Arnold Toynbee (agent): "I'll do Rip Van Winkle coming down the mountain."

Result. Professor Murray: "Oh, I've got this. It's an old sort of gnome-like person with a matted beard coming down—very funny feeling expecting to be known and find things—Oh, it's Rip Van Winkle."

The above examples were selected as typical of the most successful tests to which Professor Murray submitted. He was not always so successful as in these instances, and sometimes when the conditions were not favorable he did not have any success. But the results of the series as a whole were such that Mrs. Henry Sidgwick, in a report on the latter part of the investigations, characterized the experiments as "perhaps the most important ever brought to the notice of the Society, both on account of their frequently brilliant success and on account of the eminence of the experimenter."

From the point of view of parapsychology as an emerging branch of experimental science, some of the most significant developments of the first fifty years were those researches which represented the first efforts to investigate ESP in the setting of the university laboratory. The most striking instance was an experiment which was carried out in Holland in the Department of Psychology at the University of Groningen under the guidance of Professor M. Heymans. The principal experimental assistant was H. J. F. W. Brugmans, with whose name the experiment has become most closely associated.

Professor Brugmans later became the head of the Psychology Department in Groningen, and in 1951 Dr.

Rhine and I visited him there for a day. Professor Brugmans went over the story of how the experiment had come about. He showed us the actual rooms in their laboratory which they had used, and he brought out the musty notebooks in which they made the original records of the research. Briefly, here is the story of their adventure in research which he related.

Toward the end of World War I, a group of reserve officer students at the university had gone to see a performance by a man named Rubini whose specialty was finding objects hidden about the stage or in the audience while he was out of the room. Rubini would take the hand of someone who was in on the secret and then, without that person speaking a word, would lead him to the spot and triumphantly produce the hidden object. After the performance some of the students began trying the game among themselves in their rooms. One young officer, Van Dam, proved to be particularly successful; but his performance differed from Rubini's in one important respect—*he could find the hidden objects without having to touch anyone.*

Some of the students were so impressed with this young man's ability that they thought it should receive serious scientific study, and they reported the incident to Professor Heymans, then head of the Psychology Department. It was as Professor Heymans' assistant that Dr. Brugmans took part in the experiment planned to test the student's apparent gift for finding things.

A square hole was cut through the ceiling of one room and the floor above it, and two pieces of plate glass were fitted into the opening. A covered cubicle, or closet, was placed in the lower room. This was large enough for the subject to sit inside, and it had a slit in the front wall through which he could put his hand and let it rest on a table. There was no possible way for him to see the opening into the room above.

On the table, under the subject's hand, was placed a sort of checkerboard with 48 squares, the rows numbered 1–6 and the columns lettered A–H. For a test the experimenters in the room above would draw a numbered slip from one bag and a lettered slip from another to select a target square, and one of them would look through the window into the room below and concentrate upon having the subject "find" the right square. The subject moved his hand over the board and tapped to indicate his choice. After six tests from one room to another, the experimenters came down into the room with the subject and conducted six more tests at a close distance.

This procedure was repeated over a period of time until a total of 187 trials were completed. From the point of view of chance, the probability of the subject's being right on each trial is one in forty-eight; therefore, the expected chance number in 187 attempts is approximately 4. Actually Van Dam succeeded in getting the right square 60 times out of the 187 trials. The odds against such a result happening merely by chance are, of course, overwhelming, and you don't have to be a mathematician to see that something more than mere "luck" was involved. The success from one room to another was slightly better than that obtained with the experimenters in the same room with the subject, which argues strongly against auditory cues. Besides, the experimenters reported that even by shouting in the room above they could not make themselves heard in the room where the subject worked.

Whether this experiment, if it stood alone, would have led scientists to accept the occurrence of ESP is today merely an academic question. The results have been confirmed many times since then by tests done under even more carefully safeguarded conditions. But the Groningen ESP experiment turned out to be a one-shot contribution from that university to the cause of the psi revolution. Similarly, in a few other universities during the same general period isolated experiments were done without having this line of work become permanently established. Nowhere during the first fifty years did the seed of psi research do so well in academic soil as to yield parapsychological results on a sustained basis from a laboratory dedicated exclusively to the field. This dream, of which Professor William McDougall was the chief creator and spokesman, became a reality for the first time after Dr. Rhine came to Duke University in 1927, at the same time that Professor McDougall himself moved down from Harvard.

3

The Breakthrough in ESP:
Telepathy and Clairvoyance Differentiated

Great developments in human thought have a way of getting named after the men who played key roles in bringing them about. If the psi revolution is ever named for a particular person, it could well be called the Rhine revolution. Anyone interested in this book is bound, therefore, to be interested in Dr. J. B. Rhine.

No one can ever give a fully satisfactory answer to the question: What kind of person is John Doe? Anyone who presumes to try should start by stating his basis of acquaintance. As far as my own qualifications for speaking about Dr. Rhine are concerned, I have already said some things in Chapter 1. At this point perhaps I should say more about our early contacts as they relate to the topic of the present chapter.

I first met Dr. Rhine when I was a sophomore at Duke. I had ventured into the beginning course in psychology. Professor McDougall lectured to the entire enrollment for the first two classes of the week, and we split up into smaller quiz sections for the third meeting. Dr. Rhine was my quiz section instructor.

Our first meeting was not unusual—it gave no hint to either of us, I am sure, of what the next thirty-five years had in store for us. The only thing I remember learning in that quiz section is that the instructor was a man of extraordinary personality. He frankly told us that he himself was learning the subject with the members of the class, since he had only recently changed over from the field of botany in which he took his Ph.D. degree.

My next contact with Dr. Rhine was during the last semester of my senior year. I signed up for his course in logic. To my surprise and delight, I discovered once more that he had arranged to teach the course because he wanted to learn something about the subject himself!

One thing I remember about that course is that Dr. Rhine asked us one day to guess the numbers on cards sealed in opaque envelopes which he passed around in class. We were never told precisely what the results were, but Dr. Rhine singled out one member of the class as the star guesser. I was skeptical about the reality of ESP, but I saw the question as a proper one for scientific investigation.

The following academic year was my year of decision. During the first semester I finally faced up to the fact that my childhood choice of a career, which had carried me as far as the first semester in the School of Religion, was the wrong thing for me, personally. Dr. Rhine learned, as a result of a chance meeting on the campus, that I was struggling to make a change, and his advice played a large part in my final decision. In fact, he recommended me as a special student in the Department of Psychology to finish out that academic year.

Since I had no regular stipend for that semester of graduate work in psychology, Dr. Rhine's question whether I would like to become his research assistant in ESP was, as I said earlier, a welcome one for financial reasons as well as from the scientific point of view.

By that time (January 1932) an active and exciting program of ESP work under Dr. Rhine's supervision was already in full swing. He first started working in collaboration with his colleagues on the psychology faculty. Professor McDougall had urged that all the members of the department get behind this effort to see if this pioneering branch of investigation could be successfully transplanted into the setting of the university laboratory. They had done so for a time to the extent that their interest and their other commitments would allow. But that phase did not last long.

Dr. Rhine then started ESP work with some of his students who had become interested in this new scientific venture. He encouraged them to test themselves or their friends. Out of these efforts there soon emerged striking results. There was thus no lack of encouragement for pressing on with the research. Dr. Rhine himself, of course, also conducted ESP tests, especially when a promising subject was found. For example, he always tried to follow up with the outstanding scorers in his classroom tests. Some of these students quickly lost their ability to score above chance. Others simply would not, for personal reasons, co-operate further. A few of them went on to become star ESP subjects.

But before we continue the story of those exciting first years of ESP research at Duke, it is necessary to say a bit about the experimental *methods*. For the purposes of this book, the topic can be treated informatively without being made technical.

The first investigations of ESP at Duke took up where earlier research workers had left off. Naturally, therefore, the experiments made use of the same general kinds of test materials: subjects were asked to guess concealed objects such as numbers and playing cards. But the Duke investigators soon came to recognize the importance of developing a new ESP test. This should be based upon test objects that were not already loaded with associated ideas for the subject. Numbers, for example, are not suitable because they have values; we think of them in a particular order (1, 2, 3, etc.), and certain numbers like 3 and 7 are more likely to be selected. The same objections apply to playing cards. What was needed, therefore, was some new combination of symbols for an ESP test: designs that were as nearly neutral or as nearly equal to one another as possible, yet familiar enough not to seem strange to the subject. The number of symbols should be small enough so that the subject could easily keep them in mind.

The standard test pack of twenty-five ESP cards was invented to meet these requirements. On the face of each card is a simple design. Only five designs are used. They have been slightly revised and improved over the years, but they are basically the same as the five symbols first suggested about 1930. Today ESP cards are manufactured commercially[1] with symbols in the form:

(In taking an ESP test, the subject refers to these as circle, cross, waves, square, and star, respectively.) In the standard ESP pack of twenty-five cards, there are five of each kind.

In addition to the psychological advantages of the ESP symbols, the use of the cards in standard runs of twenty-five trials offers great advantages for the testing procedure and for mathematical evaluation of the results. Merely by thoroughly shuffling the cards and cutting them behind a screen, the experimenter can easily and quickly convert the pack into an unknown order of twenty-five random "events." The subject may then attempt to identify each card in turn by extrasensory perception when the experimenter separates it from the pack back of the screen. In the test the subject makes one and only one call for each card. Since on each trial he chooses *one* from among the *five* ESP symbols, he has—by chance—a one-fifth probability of being right. It is easy to see, therefore, that the most likely chance score for the entire run of twenty-five cards is five hits. This is the figure we get when all the one-fifth probability values of the individual cards are added up for the entire set of twenty-five cards.

Now chance scores, such as those found when shuffled

[1] The authorized distributor is Haines House of Cards, Norwood, Ohio. Each pack contains instructions for testing ESP and evaluating the results.

packs of ESP cards are compared with one another to see how often the same symbols appear in the same positions in the two random arrangements, do not always come out dead on 5. With purely chance scores, the *average* number of hits expected in a series of runs is always the number of runs multiplied by 5 (chance expectation for one run). And the sum of scores due to chance in a number of runs will vary up or down from this average chance level as we have said that they will do in individual runs. But there is a limit to how far we can reasonably expect them to vary by chance. We can use statistical tests to find out whether a total score obtained in an ESP test is far enough above or below the chance average to exceed this limit. In other words, the use of statistics tells us that we would have to repeat a chance series a specified number of times on the average to find one score as large as or larger than the one we are evaluating. This number of times that a series of trials needs to be repeated, on the average, for random fluctuations alone to produce a particular score (or a higher one) *one time* we may conveniently call the chance odds.

What do we do when we test a subject's ESP ability by having him go through a number of ESP runs? *Precisely this:* we measure his total number of hits in terms of the spread or deviation which it shows from the chance average score for that number of runs. Then we find out how likely his results would be as compared with the fluctuation of scores that chance alone should produce. In other words, we literally examine his results as if they were nothing but a matter of pure chance. We do this by applying well-known statistical methods that are widely used in science. In this way we arrive at the odds which tell us how often chance would give a total score as far away from the chance level as the one our subject has obtained.

When the chance odds at which we arrive by our statistics are as unlikely as 1 in 100, scientists generally agree that it is not reasonable to say that chance alone was involved. Therefore we reject chance and look for some lawful principle at work in the experiment. And when the odds at which the chance explanation could be invoked are even more heavily weighted against the "mere luck" hypothesis, such as 1 in 1000 or 1 in 1,000,000, it is simply not scientifically justifiable to dismiss a finding as due to pure chance.

A good ESP experimental procedure is one in which, in case the results obtained give odds that make it necessary to reject the chance hypothesis, the safeguarding conditions of the test leave no alternative explanation except ESP.

The present book will not go into technical questions of how the results of psi tests are evaluated. (I plan to write a second book on parapsychology in Russia and around the world, and I can more appropriately go into the necessary technical matters there.) But rest assured that there is nothing special or tricky about the mathematics that were used for the evaluation of the experiments described in the present volume. Just keep in mind the fact that, when the chance odds are as unlikely as 1 in 100, by ordinary scientific standards we should say that something beyond chance was involved.

It is, actually, the statement of the chance odds that

is the final objective of every statistical test. There is general agreement among scientists regarding the level which the odds should reach before they can be taken as indicating that the chance hypothesis is not reasonable and that some other explanation (such as ESP) is necessary, and this agreement gives an enormous advantage in the discussion and interpretation of experimental results. When in the pages ahead I merely cite the odds to indicate the outcome of statistical evaluations, I will be calling your attention to the real pay-off point of the experiments.

Having in mind this much about the basic ESP test methods and having decided that we can, in the present volume, travel light statistically, we can now pick up again the story of the developments on the research front itself.

My assignment as Dr. Rhine's assistant was to take a pack of ESP cards, paper, and pencil and test my friends and acquaintances on the Duke campus to see if I could find any promising subjects. He suggested that I test for *clairvoyance*: the subject should try to name the cards correctly without anyone knowing what they were at the time.

This choice of method did not seem unusual to me at the time, since I was not then well read in the history of research in this field. Thus I did not recognize that this method ran counter to an assumption which had been made in almost all of the ESP tests conducted during the first fifty years of research in the field. The investigators during that period had assumed that ESP, if it occurs, must involve a transfer of thought from one person to another—that is, that *telepathy* is the basic form of all ESP. They had, therefore, conducted most of their experiments without bothering either to take account of or to exclude the possibility of clairvoyance. Their standard procedure was to have an *agent* or *sender* look at whatever it was that the subject was trying to guess. If the subject's success was beyond the reasonable limits of chance fluctuation, the experimenters assumed that the findings proved that *telepathy* had worked.

The most distinctive advance introduced by Dr. Rhine in the first research at Duke was the use of methods to distinguish between telepathy and clairvoyance. In pure telepathy tests, *no physical cards were used.* The sender simply thought of the ESP symbols in haphazard order. He didn't even make any written record of what he was trying to "send" until the subject had made his call. In the clairvoyance tests, on the other hand, as I have already said, no one knew what the cards were until the subject had finished his calls for the run.

By the time I became active in the research, it had already become apparent that ESP results in tests for clairvoyance were as good as they were in tests for telepathy. Here was an advance in knowledge about ESP that opened up a whole new area for scientific exploration—that of clairvoyance. This breakthrough obviously had revolutionary implications from a theoretical point of view. It also promised to revolutionize the experiments from the purely practical point of view! The discovery that subjects were able to name hidden cards by ESP made it possible to use better safeguards in the testing procedures. In the telepathy tests, the possibility of some kind of undetected signaling between the sender and the subject had haunted the experimenters throughout the first fifty years. In a test for clairvoyance, in which *no one knew what the target was*, this danger was automatically eliminated. Understandably, therefore, the Duke work distinguishing between clairvoyance and telepathy inaugurated a new era in parapsychology—an era in which clairvoyance experiments have played a predominant role.

This general statement, true though it is, does not mean that to distinguish between telepathy and clairvoyance was a simple matter or that it was settled for all time by the early Duke ESP results. Indeed, the question came up again after the research had advanced to a further stage, and some of the complication encountered as a result of the experimental proof of precognition (or ESP of future events) will be described in Chapter 6.

Even today there is a strong tendency to interpret psi results in terms of telepathy if this is possible. But for the present we can let the issue rest where it stands. Not only did the Duke work show that telepathy and clairvoyance were both equally demonstrable generally as forms of ESP, but what is more, every one of the eight major subjects reported by Dr. Rhine in his first book was successful in demonstrating both forms of ESP.

This work, as I have said, initiated the era of clairvoyance in ESP research. From here on we shall be dealing with clairvoyance tests unless it is made clear that the experiment was one for pure telepathy or one for "general extrasensory perception" (GESP). The latter refers to tests in which a sender looks at a target, and hence either telepathy or clairvoyance, or both, might be involved.

My first efforts to find someone who showed promise as an ESP subject were disappointing. Over a period of two or three months I tested about a dozen people. The greatest number of trials were done with the person who was always available—myself! Nothing happened in these tests to lessen my skepticism.

Then we discovered Hubert Pearce.

Dr. Rhine told me one day that he had given a talk to the members of the School of Religion and afterward Hubert had stayed on with those students who had questions to ask. Dr. Rhine noticed that Hubert hung back until everyone else was gone, then he asked his question in a way that suggested that he had a special interest in ESP. When Dr. Rhine asked him if this was the case, the answer was yes.

Further questioning by Dr. Rhine brought out the facts that Hubert thought he might be gifted in ESP but that he was not happy with the thought of being tested. His interest, indeed, was due not so much to his own experiences along these lines as to things which he had seen his mother do. Hubert reported that she was remarkable not only for her psychic experiences but for her unusual physical powers as well. Hubert said he had seen his mother place her hands lightly on one end of a heavy, solid oak table while some men tried to hold the other end to keep it from rising from the floor. His mother had warned them that if they did not release the table it would break. Hubert said that he had seen it buckle and split across the middle!

With some reassurance from Dr. Rhine, Hubert seemed willing to have me test him for ESP. When I did this shortly afterward in Hubert's dormitory room, it was apparent that here was someone unique in my limited experience as an ESP researcher. He began, almost from the start, to score around 10 hits per run, just twice the chance level. I had no sophistication at that time about the intricacies of statistical evaluation, but I didn't need it. The background of chance scores from myself and my other subjects was enough to tell me that Hubert had something.

For the first few sessions we continued to work in Hubert's dormitory room. Then Hubert met me in Dr. Rhine's laboratory, located at that time in the Medical School Building on the Duke West Campus. Hubert adjusted to the shift of location without faltering in his ESP performance. Next Dr. Rhine took over some of the testing. Hubert kept right on with his double-chance rate.

Over the next eighteen months Dr. Rhine and I shared the work of testing this subject for clairvoyance under a wide variety of conditions with the cards in the same room. We frequently used screens to shield the cards entirely from his view. Dr. Rhine did one series in which he used entirely new packs, discarding each one after only one run, to guard against the possible criticism that Hubert might be cleverly marking the cards or performing some sort of sleight of hand.

Safe drugs were used to see if the scores could be made to go down, and up again, at will. They could: sodium amytal having the lowering effect and caffein bringing the number of hits back to the usual high level.

The climax of this period was the time when Hubert

got all twenty-five cards right in one run. Dr. Rhine had offered him $100 if the first call was a hit, then another $100 for making a hit on each of the next twenty-four trials in turn. Hubert earned the full $2500! (There was a tacit understanding that the offer was only a figurative one; Hubert did not press his claim, and Dr. Rhine admits that he has never paid.)

When Hubert returned to Duke from his summer ministerial duties in the fall of 1933, Dr. Rhine asked me to take charge of the first test of this subject's ESP when he was separated from the cards by a greater distance than one or two rooms. As a graduate student in psychology, I had a laboratory in the old Physics Building on the West Campus. Hubert had a study cubicle in the library stacks, on the side of the library away from the Physics Building. We decided to take advantage of this general situation to try some ESP tests at a distance of approximately a hundred yards.

Each day when we planned to work, Hubert would come by my room shortly before the time agreed upon for the test. We compared our watches and set them together, even allowing for the difference between the second hands. Then I watched Hubert walk across the campus and disappear into the library.

I selected a pack of ESP cards, shuffled it thoroughly, cut it, and placed it face down on the near right-hand corner of a card table at which I had taken my seat. At the time agreed upon for starting the test, I picked up the top card from the pack and, without looking at it, placed it face down on a book in the center of the table. After one minute I removed that card and placed it, still face down and still unknown to myself, at the far left-hand corner of the table and immediately placed the next card from the pack on the book.

Proceeding in this way, I placed the twenty-five cards, one after the other, on the book, leaving each one there for a minute. Meanwhile Hubert, at his study table in the library, wrote his call for each card sometime during the minute it was on the book in the center of the table. When all the cards had taken their turn on the book, I made a record of the twenty-five cards in the order in which they had been used.

As a rule, we went through this procedure again on the same day after taking a recess of five minutes to allow time for me to make the record and shuffle and cut the cards for the next run.

When the day's work was finished, Hubert and I, before we moved from our places of working, made copies of our lists of calls and cards, respectively. (These were for our own personal checkup in case we met later during the day.) Then each of us immediately sealed up the original copy of his record in an envelope, signed his name, put the date on the outside, and kept this sealed record of his part of the day's results in his own possession until he could hand it over to Dr. Rhine directly.

Hubert's level of success on the first two days in this experiment was below his usual level, but then he recovered and went on from there with run scores that were even better than the double-chance level that he had maintained with the cards in the same room. In fact, the scores on the twelve runs which we did at a hundred yards were: 3, 8, 5, 9, 10, 12, 11, 11, 12, 13, 13, 12. These scores add up to a total of 119 hits where 60 is the most likely chance number. You may still choose the chance explanation if you insist, but you would have less than 1 chance in 100,000,000,000,000 of being right! Since it is not reasonable to invoke the chance explanation against such heavy odds, we are bound to find some other interpretation. The conditions appear to leave ESP as the only possibility.

In a second subseries, I moved up to Dr. Rhine's laboratory in the Medical School and Hubert continued to work in the library. This increased the distance to approximately two hundred and fifty yards. In the forty-four runs which we did at this distance a curious effect appeared. The subject still got more *high* scores than could reasonably be attributed to chance, but he intermixed with these good runs others on which his scores were *too low to be easily written off as mere coincidence.* It seemed, in other words, as if ESP was helping him to hit the cards in some runs, but was working in reverse to make him miss them in other runs. These forty-four scores, in order, were: 1, 4, 4, 4, 7, 6, 5, 0, 6, 3, 11, 9, 0, 6, 8, 6, 9, 4, 10, 6, 11, 9, 5, 12, 7, 7, 12, 10, 6, 3, 10, 10, 6, 12, 2, 6, 12, 12, 4, 4, 3, 0, 13, 10. In spite of the up-and-down character of the scoring, the hits on these runs still add up to 75 more than the most likely chance number, and the chance odds are 1 in 1,000,000—highly significant by any scientific standards!

To see if the up-and-down swings were due to the greater distance, Hubert and I carried out a further subseries at a hundred yards, with me back at my original stand. The mixture of high and low scores went right on to a degree showing that we were faced with some *psychological* factor, not an effect of distance as such. We decided to stop the experiment to allow the subject time to recover from the bad effects of what had become a painfully monotonous task.

Professor McDougall had followed the results of the earlier stages of the experiment with great interest, but he had warned Dr. Rhine that some skeptical scientists would prefer to believe that Hubert and I had been in collusion rather than accept the results as proof of ESP. Therefore, after a rest of several months, a final subseries was done with Dr. Rhine himself present to watch over my part of the testing procedure and to see that Hubert went to his station and did not return until after each day's work with his call record in his hands. In this final, two-experimenter part of the experiment, there were only six runs, but these gave the scores: 12, 3, 10, 11, 10, 10. These results were quite enough by themselves, considering the high average rate of success, to throw the chance hypothesis out the window. The likelihood that they occurred merely as a lucky coincidence is less than 1 in 1,000,000!

When the results of the seventy-four runs in this experiment (unselfishly, Dr. Rhine labeled it the Pearce-Pratt Series, and it has come to be known by this name) are considered as a whole, the chance odds are 1 in 10,000,000,000,000,000,000,000,000. Is it any wonder that, when Dr. Rhine in 1936 described this experiment and the results in a talk at Hunter College in New York, a highly skeptical member of the Psychology Department questioned him sharply—so sharply, in fact, that Dr. Rhine impatiently said that his challenger was virtually calling him a liar and was one of those persons who would never accept ESP unless he proved it to himself in his own experiment?

Shortly after this experiment was finished, Hubert lost his ability to score above chance in the card tests. This happened rather suddenly, when he came into the laboratory one day and said he had received very disturbing news from home.

The Reverend Hubert Pearce then took up his profession as a Methodist minister in his home state of Arkansas. He has written to Dr. Rhine from time to time. In the fall of 1959 I visited him in Paris, Arkansas, and we tried some more ESP tests but with no success. This visit served to renew our friendship but it did not, alas, revive our professional partnership!

Two years after finishing the Pearce-Pratt Series, I was in New York. As I mentioned earlier, Dr. Gardner Murphy had invited me to spend two years with him at Columbia to see if we could get ESP results there comparable to those found at Duke.

One day, when Dr. Murphy and I were in his office, in walked one of his graduate students with someone who was a stranger to me, Dr. Bernard Riess of the Psychology Department at Hunter College. The following conversation—as well as my vivid memory of the occasion can reproduce it—then took place between Dr. Murphy and Dr. Riess:

Dr. Murphy: "Oh, I've been wanting to see you. I hear that you've been doing some ESP tests at Hunter."

Dr. Riess: "Well, not exactly at Hunter, but I have been doing something with a subject out in White Plains, where I live."

"How did you come to get started with ESP testing?"

"I heard Dr. Rhine speak on the subject at Hunter College. After his talk I asked him about a distance experiment which he reported and I said I couldn't believe the facts were as represented. Dr. Rhine then publicly challenged me to try some tests myself, so in my class the next day, when the students suggested that I should take up the challenge, I asked if any of them felt that they had any psychic gifts and would like to volunteer as ESP subjects. One of the students said he knew a family in White Plains the members of which seemed to be particularly gifted. For example, they always won when they played anagrams with their friends. He thought that the daughter of the family especially ought to be tested. It happened that the family lived only a quarter of a mile from my home. I made the acquaintance of this young lady and found that she was interested, and we started doing card tests in the evenings. I handled the cards in my own study and she called them in her home, and we generally went through two packs in the evening each time we worked. I used the procedure followed in the distance work at Duke, except that I turned the cards over and looked at the symbol while the subject was trying to receive her impression."

"Did you get any good results?"

"Too good."

"How is that?"

"Well, the first night the subject got scores of 5 and

7, which was near chance and just what I expected; but the second night her scores were 10 and 12. I was puzzled by such an unusual streak of luck but thought that further work would surely pull her average down to about 5. In the third session, however, she got scores of 15 and 8, and after that the lowest score she ever hit until we had done seventy-four runs, the same number as in the Duke series, was 13. She averaged over 18 hits per run of twenty-five trials over the entire series."

"Well, with results like that, what did you think?"

"I didn't know what to think, and I still don't; but you can be sure that I took precautions to insure that everything was on the level, such as working with the blinds drawn and being careful that no one could see anything even if they tried to peek in the window. I never once told the subject what her scores were, but only said that the results were interesting and that I hoped she would continue."

"Where are your records now? I would certainly be interested to see the data."

"I gave them to Dr. Zubin, the statistician up at the Medical Center. He said he thought he might find the explanation in some sort of rhythm or pattern if he could study the original records."

"Aren't you afraid your data might get lost if you let them get out of your hands?"

"I hope they do! Heaven knows there is no room for such results in my scientific philosophy!"

After this occasion brought his work to the attention of the parapsychologists, Dr. Riess showed himself to be a true scientist in his further actions regarding these unexpected and unwanted findings. He accepted the invitation of the editors of the *Journal of Parapsychology* to publish a research report on his experiment. When this report aroused interest in the full details, he published a second report in which he gave the complete records of the subject's calls and of the targets for the seventy-four runs or 1850 trials in the series.

At a symposium which was organized by the American Psychological Association for its annual convention in 1938, there was an interesting sequel to this experiment. That symposium was organized by Dr. J. L. Kennedy, at that time one of the most outspoken critics of the ESP research. Dr. Kennedy himself read a paper and served as chairman of the symposium, and he was quoted in the public press before the meeting as saying that he was ready to drive the last nail in the coffin for ESP. (Looking back on this occasion, one might be excused for observing that he must have driven that last nail before he got ESP in the coffin!) It turned out that the only thing that got buried at that A.P.A. symposium was the fashion for engaging in outspoken criticism of ESP. After that, for years the attitude of the psychologists toward the research was more nearly one of studied neglect. After all the uproar of the preceding years, the decline in criticism seemed like stony silence!

During the discussion period at the A.P.A. meeting, the chairman said that he had been asked by Dr. Murphy to call upon Dr. Riess of Hunter College to tell about the conditions of his experiment. Dr. Riess spoke to his professional colleagues in the following words:

"There is nothing much to say. This subject worked

for me awhile last year, made seventy-four runs, and then stopped because of her condition of health. She had a sort of general breakdown. She has since, unfortunately, disappeared into the Middle West and at present is not available for further work. So far as errors in recording are concerned, I hear Dr. Murphy found one error, and I owe him ten dollars for finding that one. But with that error eliminated, the only other error that may have crept in is a possibility of deception, and the only person who could have done the deceiving is myself since the subject at no time knew how well she was doing nor had any idea of the cards which were being turned by myself in my room a quarter of a mile away from where she was working. Outside of that there can be no criticism of the method used. I had the deck of cards on my desk, shuffled them, and at the stated time turned them over one by one, making a record of each card. I had my desk piled with examination papers and half the time I don't think I was conscious of any serious concentration on my part. I kept the records locked up in my desk and some-times it was a week before I totaled up the scores and found the number of high scores she was making. In-cidentally, the whole thing started when a group of students at Hunter College wanted to do some of the ex-periments. I undertook the experiment as a way of dem-onstrating to my classes that ESP did not occur. I did not succeed in that. I had sixty-seven other students who worked for me, none of whom had an average score above 5 [of any significance]. So I was left with one case. After I got the data collected and found that the subject aver-aged around 18, I did not know what to do but publish the results. I do not know whether Dr. Britt [who had spoken critically about ESP earlier in the discussion] believes in throwing away good data just because he doesn't precisely understand the full implications of those data, but I felt that they should be reported."

This is the most spectacular experiment in which a research worker has been convinced of the genuineness of ESP by his own results and against his own wishes, but Dr. Riess is only one of a number of investigators in this category. Indeed, I count myself among these, though my conversion came while I was still a student and before I had announced my skepticism. But another spectacular example of an experimenter who had to eat crow publicly when he found that his own results proved ESP was Dr. S. G. Soal of London University.

Dr. Soal's interest in parapsychology dates back to the years following World War I. He had some experiences with a medium which convinced him of the genuineness of telepathy, but for a long time all of his efforts to obtain results in quantitative tests were unsuccessful. After the publication of Dr. Rhine's first book in 1934, Mr. Soal (he received his doctor's degree only later as a result of his experiments in ESP) became known as the most outspoken critic of the Duke ESP experiments. He announced that he was going to set aside three years to see if the American results could be repeated in England, and during the course of that period he announced several times that his experiments were yielding only chance results. The implication was that his failure to find evidence of ESP somehow undermined the conclusions of the American investigators who had obtained and published their positive results.

But as things turned out, this negative conclusion of Dr. Soal's proved to be premature. In 1940 he was persuaded by another English investigator to take a further and closer look at the records from 160 subjects he had tested to see if one or more of these individuals showed a peculiar type of effect which the second investigator had noticed in his own ESP experiments. The question was: Were any of Dr. Soal's subjects actually using ESP but scattering their aim over more than one target in a way that caused the experimenter to overlook their success? Had any of them made a significantly extra-chance number of hits on the cards coming just before or just after the ones designated as the targets? In taking this further look at his results, Dr. Soal examined first the data of two subjects who had been the most interesting to him. Both of these subjects did indeed show this "displacement" type of scoring! The rate of hitting on the targets coming just before or after the one at which a sender was looking during each trial was so high that the chance explanation was completely unreasonable!

If his work had ended at that point, this finding would have remained as simply a challenging puzzle. But the work with these two subjects did not end there. One of them was available for two years of experiments carried out in London during the war and at the height of the German bombings. In this series of experiments Dr. Soal formed a research partnership with Mrs. Mollie Goldney, another member of the Society for Psychical Research in London, and the two of them tested the subject, Basil Shackleton, under safeguarding conditions designed to meet every conceivable type of criticism short of the ridiculous. Over this two-year period the subject's rate of hitting was about thirty per cent of the trials, where chance would yield approximately twenty per cent. The work as a whole had odds for occurring by chance one time in a million billion billion billion repetitions of such a series. By varying the conditions, the investigators found and were able to study a number of conditions that influenced the rate of scoring.

With Mrs. Gloria Stewart, his second subject, Dr. Soal and Mr. F. Bateman, his colleague and the co-author of the book included in the list at the end of this volume, did experiments over a period of four and a half years, from 1945 until 1950. When Mrs. Stewart began these tests (ten years after her first ESP tests, in which she showed displacement) she was successful in making her hits on the actual target for each trial, instead of on the target before or after it as she had done previously. Her rate of success was about the same as Mr. Shackleton's and, because the number of trials was larger, the chance odds were even more overwhelming.

By the time Dr. Soal did his work, the question of evidence for the occurrence of ESP was no longer one of real importance for the investigators. Since about 1940 we had been primarily interested in varying the test conditions for clues to the nature of the subject's ESP ability. There is no definable point in time when the evidence became strong enough to establish once and for all the reality of ESP as a fact of nature. This time undoubtedly has varied from individual to individual. But most workers in the field agreed with Dr. Robert H. Thouless when he said in his presidential address to the Society for Psychical Research in 1942 that the ". . . point has, I think, been passed [when] the reality of the phenomena must be regarded as proved as certainly as anything in scientific research can be proved."

Long before that time, as I have indicated, many research workers thought of their efforts as being directed more at gaining a better understanding of ESP than at simply re-proving its existence. As the research has gone on apace the literature has grown enormously. It is no longer possible for one book or two—indeed, not even a dozen!—fully to summarize the basic evidence for psi and the findings that mark at least the beginnings of new knowledge about it already available in the scientific literature of parapsychology.

A few facts will serve to illustrate how broad the general topic of ESP alone has become. In 1937 a scientific journal was first issued at Duke University—the *Journal of Parapsychology.* It has been published without interruption since that date, and all twenty-six volumes have been devoted primarily to reports of original research. And this is only one of four journals in this field in the English language. In 1940 the members of the research staff of the Duke Parapsychology Laboratory co-operated in publishing a book with the title, *Extrasensory Perception after Sixty Years.* This volume, an evaluation of the evidence for ESP as it then stood, contained more than 400 pages of facts and figures and summarized the results of 145 experimental reports. The work done during the past twenty-three years represents more psi experiments than were done during the first sixty years covered in that survey.

My purpose in mentioning these things is not to frighten you with what you must be prepared to read in the present book. Rather, it is to explain that this book cannot possibly give the entire history of the psi revolution. Here, the most that I can do is to give you some feeling of acquaintance with the moments of high drama which have marked the progress of this research throughout more than eighty years of its history, and especially of those incidents which have been most dramatic for me personally—the particular historic events which I was privileged to observe at first hand.

A further popular account of just what has been achieved in this field of research so far and how things stand with parapsychology around the world is reserved, as I have said, for discussion in a second book. But I cannot end this chapter without mentioning briefly some of the things that have been reported that bear upon questions about the nature of ESP. Some of the findings regarding the nature of other psi phenomena must, of course, be left for later chapters in which those forms of psi will be discussed.

An important part of the breakthrough in ESP was the realization that this ability is a normal one. It is not necessary for an investigator to wait until he finds a rare and special subject. One can start by looking for ESP ability in himself, then in the members of his immediate family and among his friends and acquaintances.

The general assumption made by the ESP researchers of the past three decades is that everyone most probably has this ability. Success in demonstrating it depends more upon the psychological conditions of the test than upon the person used as subject. Nor need anyone fear that he is in any way abnormal in case he *does* prove to be outstanding in his ESP performance. On the contrary, ESP success is associated with normal, healthy attitudes of mind rather than the reverse.

Just as a subject requires special conditions to demonstrate his ESP abilities, so also does an experimenter need special skill in handling him to enable him to continue. In fact, this skill of maintaining the right conditions has not yet been fully mastered by the research workers. As a consequence, subjects have tended to grow stale or become "uninspired" as the testing continued. It has been the rule that outstanding subjects sooner or later lose their ability to score above the chance level. This fact has been a major source of discouragement and difficulty for the experimenters, but it is at the same time a challenge to press on with the research. This fact does *not* mean that the significance of the outstandingly successful experiments may be called into question. It does, however, indicate how incomplete as yet is our knowledge of psi and it challenges us to search all the harder for an approach or a special state of mind that will give us real control over these elusive abilities.

ESP appears to be related to intelligence but only in an indirect way. That is, comparisons of ESP and IQ scores have shown only a slight positive correlation. This rather suggests that, among the school students who were involved in these studies, the more intelligent ones more readily grasped the nature and purpose of the ESP test and therefore were able to do better on it.

ESP does not appear to belong to one cultural, racial, age, or sex division of the human race more than to the others. Spontaneous psi experiences have been reported from every age of recorded history and from every region on the face of the earth where an interest has been shown in such matters. Likewise, the experimental investigation of ESP has shown no consistent favoring or disfavoring of any special subgroup of the species of *Homo sapiens.*

There is even good reason to ask whether ESP does not also occur in animals, as we shall see in Chapters 8 and 9 of this book.

An important grouping of findings is concerned with the question of where ESP fits into the general personality. We face first of all the indications that it has no specific organic or nervous-system localization; no characteristic "feeling" such as we associate with the senses of sight, hearing, smell, taste, touch, and the like. In fact, there seems to be no way that the individual can identify the occurrence of ESP in himself in terms of any distinguishing feeling for the process that sets it off from pure guessing. Time after time, subjects have tried to say when their ESP was operating in a test, to pick out their correct calls. They have as a rule done no better when they claimed success than when they did not. Thus as far as the laboratory tests are concerned the subject is basically unconscious of when he is using ESP.

One of the consequences of the fact that ESP works on the unconscious level is that subjects sometimes use this ability to bring about a result just the reverse of what they are trying to achieve. We saw some evidence of this in the unusually large number of *low* scores in the second subseries of the Pearce-Pratt Series. Of the large number of experiments done both before and after that time, many have produced compelling evidence that this unwanted reversal in scoring—what the experimenters have named psi-missing—does take place.

Psi-missing has been noted, for example, in a long series of experiments carried out by Dr. Gertrude Schmeidler, a psychologist on the faculty of City College of New York. Dr. Schmeidler, over the course of several years, would describe a clairvoyance experiment to the members of her classes, and then ask the students, before they took the ESP test, to indicate their attitude. Did the students think they could do better than chance or were they open-minded to this possibility? (Subjects who put themselves in this category were called "sheep.") Or did they reject outright the possibility of showing any ESP ability? (If so, they were called "goats.") After the experimenter had collected the records of the ESP tests, she was able to separate the sheep from the goats. She found that the sheep consistently scored above the expected chance level; *but the goats scored significantly below chance.*

Other research workers have been especially interested in other ways in which the attitudes of those taking part in the tests, both experimenter and subjects, seem to influence the outcome of the ESP test. We began to suspect quite early in the Duke ESP research during the thirties that the *experimenter* may make all the difference between success or failure of the test. Ironically, I proved to be a Jonah for ESP subjects when I first returned to the Parapsychology Laboratory after my two years in New York. During the time I had been away, the "policy" in the laboratory had shifted in a subtle but nevertheless, for me, quite significant way. All my own efforts up to that time and such slight success as had attended them had come as a result of first looking for a promising subject. Once he was spotted in exploratory tests I selected him for special attention and special study in individual ESP tests. This was (as I believe) the way I had first worked successfully with Hubert Pearce, and it was the method which I had followed implicitly during my stay in New York.

When I returned to Duke, however, I found that it was no longer considered proper to be concerned with the question of whether one had a promising high-scoring subject for his experiments. Rather, the approach that was favored at that time and in the years since was to start with an interesting problem that one wanted to solve in the research. Having a suitable problem, it was assumed, one could test all comers with confidence; and given the right psychological conditions, a sufficiently large number of the subjects would show enough ESP to make the total results significant. Thus the experimenter would reach the desired solution of his problem without having to search for good subjects.

This approach worked well for some members of the laboratory research staff, as well as for some in other centers who were doing ESP experiments—but not for me! Within the short span of one semester, my reputation as a Jonah among experimenters was firmly established. And with good reason, for I was going once a week with another member of the staff to a neighboring city to test children in special situations: first, in a school for the blind; then in an orphanage. Week after week my colleague came back to Duke with highly significant results, while I came home empty-handed.

So we planned an experiment to see if there was really a difference between us, as ESP experimenters, even though we were following the same general approach in the research. The experiment lent support to this idea. We combined forces and began to work as a team to test the same subjects and we got good results when my partner, Miss Peggy Price, talked to the subject and set the stage for the the test (while I sat, watching like a hawk, in the background). But when I tried to prepare the psychological situation for the ESP test while Peggy looked on in silence, we drew a complete blank!

Our report of this little experiment has become a classic in the research on ESP as the first effort to test the firm conviction (which many of the research workers had already formed) that the investigator is an important influence in the test—something that can make all the difference between evidence of ESP and no ESP!

Many years later this same point came into the research in a somewhat different way. Miss Margaret Anderson (now Dr. Anderson) had come to the Parapsychology Laboratory at Duke because she was interested, as a public school teacher, in the question of whether there was something to be explored about the teacher-pupil relationship in the classroom that went beyond the questions one could learn about by reading textbooks in educational psychology. She was interested, in other words, in the possibility that there might be an ESP factor in the teaching situation.

To test her idea, Dr. Anderson got the co-operation of a number of classroom teachers across the country. She also joined forces with Miss Rhea White as a co-experimenter in the Duke laboratory. Then they prepared test materials which the teachers could give to each pupil in their classes. The materials for the individual test for clairvoyance were mainly a record sheet containing several runs of targets sealed in an opaque envelope with a blank record stapled to the outside for the subject's calls. But Dr. Anderson and Miss White did not simply test for ESP. The pupils were asked to answer a questionnaire revealing what they really thought of the teacher. They had a full guarantee that the teacher would not learn how they answered. In turn, the teacher indicated whether or not he liked each pupil.

True to the indications from the results of other researchers, and just as Dr. Anderson suspected from her classroom experience, it turned out that those pupils who liked the teacher scored significantly above chance on the average in their ESP test, while those who did not like the teacher scored significantly below the chance level. In a similar manner, those students whom the teacher liked scored high, while those that the teacher did not like scored below chance. Does this mean that science is near the point of discovering what so many have known intuitively for so many centuries? Are some teachers and some pupils "right" for each other because of some subtle state of mind related to ESP? May parapsychology yet find that one of its realms of practical application is that most important of all areas of human endeavor, the art of teaching, without which our culture could not survive from one generation to another? These queries serve to illustrate the fact that successful research always raises a whole series of new questions in the place of every one it answers. Thus the pursuit of knowledge is an endless task, and no one need hesitate in choosing parapsychology as a career for fear of working himself out of a job!

I hope it is clear that the first big breakthrough in ESP—distinguishing between clairvoyance and telepathy—has borne fruit in other breakthroughs. Nor must you suppose that the present chapter has a monopoly on the breakthroughs that followed from the truly significant advance in research in parapsychology achieved by the first golden years in the Duke laboratory. The topics that will claim our attention in the remaining chapters of this book have all grown directly out of the developments of those exciting days, and the forward thrust of that research is still making itself felt. Who knows? Perhaps what has transpired in parapsychology until now has been only the preparation for a new breakthrough, one that could advance the psi revolution to a position of honor and favor comparable to that enjoyed by the atomic revolution or the space revolution!

4

Mind over Matter:
Psychokinesis in the Laboratory

Question: When a free afternoon has been provided in the middle of a four-day biological convention to give some relief from listening to technical papers, what would be better than a picnic or a sight-seeing tour?

Answer: Another scientific meeting to hear two more technical papers—by two parapsychologists invited especially for the occasion!

This, at least, was the answer the Canadian Physiological Society gave to the question when it met in Winnipeg in June 1960. Those responsible for planning the activities for the free Thursday afternoon boldly decided to schedule more of the serious business of science while the other organizations were interrupting their conventions to relax and play. The physiologists asked Dr. Gardner Murphy of the Menninger Foundation to talk on the investigation of ESP, and they invited me to speak on the laboratory research on PK (psychokinesis: the direct influence of mind upon matter).)

The members of the arrangements committee warned us before the meeting that we might be speaking largely to empty seats. To their surprise and delight, the large lecture hall was filled, and the meeting time was extended for a second hour until the chairman had to call a halt because of other scheduled activities. Those who were too interested to heed the closing gavel took Dr. Murphy and me to dinner, and about thirty of them asked us to continue the discussion, which we did until about ten o'clock in the evening.

What did we say that so captured and held their attention? Dr. Murphy's topic dealt, of course, with matters such as those already covered in Chapters 2 and 3 of this book. My own paper dealt with the research developments that will be described in the next several pages.

(Can wishing for something help to make it happen? I do not mean can it help anyone work harder to get what he wants, but can the mind somehow act to influence directly, even if to only the slightest degree, the course of physical events?)This idea is not a stranger to any of us, for we all went through the period of childhood when the heroes of fairy tales and mythology were our daily companions. We admired them when they triumphed through their good wishes, and most of us have thought of what we could do if only we were granted *our* three wishes.

Yes, you may say, but surely we left this all behind us, even long before we became adults.

But do we really outgrow this fanciful way of think-

ing? Must we accept as final truth the teachings of
modern scientists who would sentence the mind to life
imprisonment in the physical brain and who would deny
it not only any wishing power but all other powers as
well? If they are right, yes, of course we must. But if
they are *not* right in wanting to banish the power of
thought from the universe, what could be more important than using the methods of science to keep man
from literally losing his mind?

The discovery that we have abilities which allow us to
know about things happening at a distance, beyond the
reach of our senses—that is, the discovery of even the
simplest forms of ESP—may by itself be enough to prove
that mind exists. At least, no one has yet developed a
theory that succeeds in explaining telepathy and clairvoyance in purely physical terms. But scientists should
not be satisfied simply because they have demonstrated
experimentally *some* of the unique actions of mind. If
there are ways other than ESP by which its existence
may be known and its nature investigated, we must explore and attempt to explain these other psi mysteries
as well.

In daily life, the use of the senses is closely linked
with things that we do. I *see* the open box of candy
and I *reach* for a piece and *plop* it into my mouth.
You *hear* your name, and you *turn* your head to see who
is calling you. In fact, almost every instance of sensory
perception leads to some action or muscular response.

Does not this close linkage of *sensing* and *doing* in
ordinary experience justify our wondering whether the
same is not true in the realm of psi phenomena? Does

not ESP, in which the mind is directly influenced by events in the outside world, lead us to expect that PK should also occur? If you think, for example, of clairvoyance as the influence of matter upon mind, should we not find that the same general psi capacity works in the opposite direction—an effect of mind over matter?

If you feel that this line of reasoning is too far removed from daily life to be taken seriously, pay a visit to the nearest bowling alley. There you will see husky youths, hardheaded men from the workaday world of industry and finance, and practical housewives all demonstrating that they do not stop trying to influence the ball after they have released it. The bowler sways and strains to guide the ball as it moves toward the pins at the far end of the alley. True, if you ask him whether his efforts are doing any good, he is likely to say no. But the fact remains that he acts, under the stress of the moment, *as if* he is guiding the ball after it has been sent on its way. If the very idea of mind over matter is so foreign to our vaunted scientific culture, why should we all so openly fall uncritically into superstition under stress, when we forget about our inhibitions?

May the truth not be that we really *know*, in spite of all the efforts to educate us to the contrary, that the mind has a force of its own that may at times be called upon to influence a physical situation, such as a faulty bowling effort?

As long as we remember that this question will not answer itself, but that it must be decided by careful, objective, experimental research, what do we have to lose by raising the issue? For science and for mankind generally, the irreparable loss would come from mistakenly closing our eyes to the possibility that there may be something to the old and familiar idea of mind over matter, something just waiting for the right scientific method and the right moment in the advancing tide of research to be discovered.

Thomas Huxley said: "It is the customary fate of new truths to begin as heresies and to end as superstitions." But the old adage of mind over matter has long been so very prominently labeled as superstition without ever having been credited as truth that it is doubtful if it could be brought into the arena of scientific investigation through purely logical considerations alone. Fortunately, Nature herself occasionally gives us some encouragement to think that there is something to PK. Mysterious physical effects in the realm of experience, spontaneous unexplained objective events that appear to have some personal significance, do take place. These PK experiences are not so frequent as those in the area of ESP, but they are sufficiently numerous to raise the question for the psi research worker. Some of these cases from daily life were cited in Chapter 2—the stopping of a person's clock or watch or the unexplained falling of his picture from the wall at the time of his death—and they also include the examples of persistent household disturbances, the so-called poltergeist cases, with which we will be concerned in the next chapter.

Interest in PK is not new in parapsychology. Not only has the spontaneous PK occurrence long been the object of serious study, but there were decades both before and during the first fifty years when investigators seriously attempted to test the claims of individuals who were reputed to possess remarkable powers of mind over matter. Some of these studies, such as those Sir William Crookes carried out with the famous D. D. Home, were reported in the scientific literature with startling findings, and they remain even today as a challenge to the openminded explorer. But others of these earlier efforts at PK investigation became hopelessly lost in the darkness of the mediumistic séance room. Clearly, the study of PK was stalled unless and until someone could find a suitable method of tackling the problem, a method similar to the one by which ESP had been successfully brought into the laboratory.

After the first publication on the ESP research at Duke in 1934, Dr. Rhine thought that the time had come for making a new attack upon the PK problem. But how was this to be done? The answer came from a casual visitor to the Duke laboratory. He claimed that he could successfully will dice to fall so that they would give the numbers he needed in order to win. His confident boast reminded Dr. Rhine that many experienced players of the game of craps believe that they are able to control the dice.

The visitor went on his way, but he left his beautifully simple idea behind. Dr. Rhine had his method for testing PK. Both he and Mrs. Rhine, using themselves and a few friends and students as subjects, set out to see if this was the answer. The first tests were made by throwing two dice for high dice (a total of 8 or more on both faces), low dice (6 or fewer), or sevens. The first work naturally was exploratory, and the dice were thrown under a variety of circumstances. Some of the trials were made as in ordinary dice games: the cubes were shaken in cupped hands and rolled upon a blanketed surface or bounced off a "wall" before they stopped rolling. For other tests, the dice were shaken in a cup and immediately thrown blindly from it. In still others, the dice were rolled down an inclined chute onto a table or the floor.

These first PK tests yielded results that were consistently beyond the average expected by chance coincidence. The subjects maintained their success over a large number of throws and the odds against chance were very great. The experimenters, of course, had confidence in their own results, but they wanted confirmation by others before publishing such startling findings. Dr. Rhine therefore quietly informed a few people about the work and encouraged them to undertake PK tests. Several of them did so.

This stage of quiet research on the PK hypothesis lasted from 1934 through 1942. Very early during this period, variations in testing procedure were made. For example, some subjects preferred to try for a designated target face instead of the sum of the faces on a pair of dice. This kind of test was more adaptable since it allowed the subject to throw any number of dice at the same time. Tests were made with from 1 to 96 or more dice per throw. As the experiments advanced beyond the exploratory stage, adequate safeguards were introduced to control against physical bias of the dice by throwing equally for every face, and machines were made to throw the dice for trial after trial. Once the dice were put into the machine, no one touched them again until the experiment was finished.

Most of these series, like the first tests made at Duke by the Rhines, gave highly significant results. As each experiment was finished, the results were noted in terms of the over-all scores, and the records were sent to the Parapsychology Laboratory to be added to the PK file. This process continued over the eight-year period before the Duke experimenters felt that the degree of confirmation justified publication.

Then, in the course of re-examining the data before reporting the findings, the investigators discovered a new type of *internal* evidence. This discovery provided a clear-cut basis for excluding the counterhypotheses to PK even in the more exploratory series. The evidence was the observation of the fact that highly significant rhythmic changes had occurred in the level of the subject's success in relation to his progress through the PK test. By chance, of course, there is no reason to expect that one section of the record page should consistently do better than another. As the subjects worked their way through the trials that the procedure required to complete a particular unit of the test, their success had gone up and down in a remarkably regular and lawful way.

No one had anticipated or noticed this variation in performance while the tests were being conducted. Consequently no one gave any thought to such position effects. Therefore neither the experimenters nor the subjects were *consciously* motivated in one part of the record page more than in another. This discovery made it possible to consider as evidence for PK the results of exploratory experiments in which subjects threw for the face of their choice instead of trying equally for all faces to guard against any effect of physical bias in the dice. If the 6-face, say, was used as target throughout an experiment, a high total score might be due to the fact that the larger number of spots (holes) on that face made it lighter and this caused it to turn up more often. But a statistical test based upon the *difference* between the numbers of 6-faces found in two different sections of the record page could not be interpreted as something that happened because of physical bias in the dice. The 6-face would not be *favored because it is lighter* during the throws made at one particular moment and the 6-face on the same dice then be *disfavored because it is heavier* in the throws made at the next moment.

What were the unexpected position effects found in the PK records? When the first series was being reanalyzed, the investigators observed that there was a general decline of success between the top half and the bottom half of the record page. Similarly, they noticed that there was a decline of success between the data recorded in the left-hand and right-hand columns. As a means of getting a standard and optimal test of these two trends, they divided the page into four equal quarters by means of horizontal and vertical lines. Then they made a statistical evaluation of the difference in the hits scored in the upper left and the lower right quarters of the page, a test they named the "quarter distribution" or QD analysis.

Having discovered a decline effect in the first records

examined, the experimenters went on to apply the QD analysis to all of the other records already in the files. A total of eighteen separate experimental series were found to be suitable for evaluation by this method.

In twelve of these series the subjects had been throwing for a designated *face* of the die as target. In all but one of these the QD analysis showed a higher rate of scoring in the upper left quarter than in the lower right quarter of the page. Statistically, a difference as large as that observed for all twelve series between the total score of the upper left and the lower right quarters would be expected by chance one time in more than 30,000,000 such sets of data.

The other six series were experiments in which the subjects threw a pair of dice for a target *sum* of the two faces. The QD results once again showed that in all but one series the upper left quarter had given a higher score than the lower right. Here the difference between the total scores would be expected by chance one time in more than 150 such sets of records. Even this result has better than 1 in 100 chance odds, and so it is statistically significant.

The QD results for the PK record page were discovered and reported by Dr. Rhine and Miss Betty Humphrey of the Duke Parapsychology Laboratory. Seeing this new evidence as solid proof of the PK hypothesis, they issued an invitation for any qualified scientists to come and recheck the results for themselves. When no one else accepted the invitation, I took the opportunity. Although I was a member of the staff, I was away from the laboratory when their analyses were made, and thus I was qualified to make a completely separate recheck. I rechecked the ten out of the eighteen series which contributed most of the PK evidence from the QD analysis. A few minor errors of tabulation were found, but these did not make any real difference in the results. Thus my own findings verified the discovery of a lawful grouping of hits in the data that could not be written off as chance and for which there was no explanation except that of mind working with spontaneous bursts of force at the start of a new page.

The QD analysis was carried through two further stages to see if the decline effect was present in units of the records smaller than the page. The final stage was one that I suggested as a check that was completely independent statistically of the page QD that had already been found. The results of this analysis carried as much weight as they would have if a totally different set of records were being analyzed. This was a study involving the quartering of record units lying wholly *within* the four quarters of the page, a sort of quarter distribution analysis of the original page quarters.

I had originally urged that this study should be made before I had seen any of the PK data. Thus there could be no question regarding whether I had simply looked over the old records until I found something that seemed good and then had planned an analysis to take advantage of a lucky hindsight. This would not have done at all, of course. It would be like betting on a horse race after it has been run and the results were known! We were never so foolish in any of the QD analyses, but it was nice to have the results of this third study to prove the findings to the hilt.

Out of the original eighteen series, only eight were suitable for this third QD study. These showed the predicted decline effect with the odds for chance occurrence of 1 in 200,000. This study by itself was strong evidence of PK, especially for the reason that it confirmed the results previously found in the study of the QD of the page.

This is how the case for PK stood in 1945, eleven years after the first dice tests were started and three years after the publication of the first results. The case was conclusive—as conclusive, at least, as it could be on the basis of work largely centered in or directed from one laboratory. From that time, the hypothesis had scientific status, commanding the close attention of research workers in parapsychology. The question was: Could the evidence be confirmed by investigators in other research centers?

Since 1945 there have been many confirmatory PK experiments, but I will present the basic details regarding only three of them here and a fourth one involving a new type of test a bit later.

In 1946, Mrs. Laura A. Dale reported a PK experiment which she had conducted at the American Society for Psychical Research in New York. The experiment was planned from the outset to guard against every imaginable way in which non-PK factors might influence the results. Fifty-four college students were used as subjects, each one taking part in a single session. Two dice at a time were shaken in a cup and poured into the top end of a chute. They tumbled about three feet down an incline and came to rest in an enclosed area at the bottom.

Both the experimenter and the subject silently recorded the faces of the dice after each throw. The score of the entire experiment of more than 31,000 die-throws was above chance to the degree represented by odds of 1 in 200.

Another effort to repeat the PK work was made at the University of Pittsburgh. This experiment by Dr. R. A. McConnell and two associates used 393 subjects and involved about 170,000 die releases. A special feature of this experiment was the use during two thirds of the trials of an automatically operating electrical apparatus for throwing the dice. The dice, as they lay, were photographed by a camera attached to the machine and they were also recorded by the experimenter. The photographic record made it possible to recheck the scores from the films and thus to find any errors in the experimenters' records. The total score of the experiment was not significantly different from chance, but the decline effect on the record page showed a drop in scoring with chance odds of 1 in 500.

A third effort to confirm the PK work done at Duke was an experiment conducted by Mr. G. W. Fisk and Dr. D. J. West in England with a selected high-scoring PK subject. An unusual feature about this work was the fact that the subject was not informed which face of the die was the target for any given set of trials. Thus the subject had to use ESP to get the target and PK to make the dice fall to match it. The subject worked in her own home where she simply threw the dice to match the unknown targets as they were set up a number of miles away. The first series of 10,000 trials gave results above chance with odds of 1 in 625. In three further series this subject also obtained consistently positive scores under the conditions that required the use of both ESP and PK. These further results had chance odds of 1 in 5880.

The above three examples of independent confirmations of the early Duke PK results are offered here both because of the experimental conditions and because of the results. I could have chosen a number of other series with comparably well-controlled conditions that did not yield as striking results and others that did not measure up to these in safeguards but gave better scores. The PK research has not proved to be any royal road to discovery for the investigators, for in several instances they have met with success in their first experiments only to find that efforts to repeat their work were fruitless. These unsuccessful tests have been cited by some critics as grounds for discounting or rejecting the positive cases. But the real lesson they teach us is that the essential psychological conditions for getting PK to work in a test situation are difficult to provide and even harder to keep. The case for PK needs to be considered on the basis of the total evidence, not on that of one worker or one group or one period. But it is interesting to observe the extent to which the results of the second period of the research confirmed the findings of the first phase as done in or directed from the Duke laboratory. This is why I have called attention to the outstanding experiments of the period after the first announcement of the PK evidence and when the problem had been taken up in other centers. On the basis of *both* the safeguards *and* the results, the three studies described above should provide the answer to the question of any open-minded person who might wonder whether the case for PK depends entirely on work done in the Parapsychology Laboratory.

In all the work described so far the target was the face of a die or a combination of two faces. We come now to PK work that introduced a radically new departure in method—efforts to influence the placement of falling objects by PK.

In 1951, Mr. W. E. Cox reported an experiment in which subjects attempted to use PK on a tumbling die in two ways at the same time: one, to get target faces; and the other, to make the dice stop on those squares on a checkerboard surface which were marked with the target-face number. Both the target-face data and the placement data were statistically significant.

This beginning on the study of PK placement was followed up by other investigators, chiefly by Mr. Haakon Forwald, an engineer in Sweden.

Since 1951, Mr. Forwald has been the most active investigator of PK placement. By the end of 1957 he had published eight reports on his research. In this work the investigator, serving as his own subject, mechanically released cubes to roll down an inclined plane and spread out on a horizontal throwing surface. A center line divided the horizontal surface into equal right- and left-hand areas. The subject's aim was to influence the falling objects to stop on the side chosen as the target. The two sides were used as target the same number of times, and thus any physical bias in the apparatus was controlled.

During the first series, the results were scored only in

terms of the division of objects between the target and non-target sides. Nevertheless, the number of objects falling within the target area was highly significant.

Mr. Forwald then introduced a simple change in his apparatus with the purpose of achieving a more sensitive measure of the PK placement effect. He drew lines parallel to the center line of the table at one-centimeter intervals and numbered them to provide a "scale." Thereafter the cubes were scored on each throw to show the actual degree of displacement.

The experimenter released six cubes on each trial and ten releases were recorded together as a set, the first five for the right-hand or A-side of the table as target and then five for the left-hand or B-side. The data were evaluated in terms of the difference between the cube distribution when A was target and that for B as target.

As Mr. Forwald continued his research, two general facts became clear. One was that he was getting, with almost marvelous regularity, an effect upon the placement of the dice in the direction of his wishes. The second was that this effect was not uniformly distributed throughout the set, but was more concentrated in the first throw of the set for each target side. As evidence that something more than chance was operating, his data were conclusive. Because the placement effect was found in the first throw of the set, it became standard procedure in the evaluation of his data to select these results for separate analysis.

Parapsychologists have long been subjected to criticisms of a kind that scientists in other fields do not need to worry about. When any psi investigator working alone has obtained significant results, it has been commonplace to hear that he could have made errors of observation and recording and thus have deceived himself. To forestall such criticism, it was necessary for Mr. Forwald to repeat his tests in the presence of a witness and independent recorder.

This need was met in the fall of 1957 during a visit by Mr. Forwald to the Duke Parapsychology Laboratory. The purpose of the visit was tacitly understood but not overtly stressed. We recognized that any PK subject would be placed at a psychological disadvantage if he felt "put on the spot." Consequently we were interested in approaching the crucial stage of his visit by slow degrees. Dr. Rhine asked me to supervise Mr. Forwald's work at Duke, and in the end I joined Mr. Forwald in reporting the research.

As a starting point Mr. Forwald worked through two series entirely alone as he had done in Sweden. These series give significant results for the first throw of the set (the basis of the statistical test, selected in advance on the strength of his previous work), with odds of 1 in 140 and 1 in 58, respectively.

He then tried repeating this success when a member of the laboratory staff was assigned as an independent observer and recorder. Two series done under this condition were totally without statistical significance.

In the next stage, three different members of the laboratory staff in separate series participated as *co-subject* as well as independent observer and recorder. With one of these laboratory members, Mr. Forwald's results were significant, with odds of 1 in 166. So far the results were merely exploratory as far as the real purpose of the visit was concerned.

Finally plans were made for a confirmatory test set up on the basis of the work done up to that point. In this test Mr. Forwald had as his co-subject Mrs. Peggy Murphy, the member of the laboratory with whom he had previously worked most successfully in exploratory series. This member of the laboratory also made an independent record of the cubes. The two observers compared their records on the spot and reached agreement before the cubes were disturbed. The results showed a high level of significance, with odds of 1 in 5000. Thus, in spite of the psychological difficulties which had to be overcome, the Duke series confirmed this subject's abilities under conditions excluding subjective errors of observation and recording.

But Mr. Forwald's objective in his work as a whole has not been limited to piling up more and more evidence for a PK placement effect. Almost from the beginning of his research he has been trying to gain some insight into the dynamics of the PK process. He has, for example, compared cubes of different kinds of materials, weights, roughness, and surface coatings. At the same time he has worked out mathematical formulas for converting the effect obtained (taking into account the relevant aspects both of the cube movements and of the cubes themselves) into the physical energy equivalents for bringing about the result. It is too soon to attempt to make any general scientific evaluation of these research efforts, since they are still at an early stage of development. I mention them only as an indication of the fact that the investigators of the PK effect are aware of the need to find ways of relating this function to more familiar scientific principles. Parapsychologists not only want to know whether PK occurs; as soon as this conclusion is reached, they turn to the much more difficult task of trying to learn something about the nature of the effect.

Other investigators have also continued to contribute to the study of the PK placement effect during the past decade. There has been further research from Mr. Cox, who was the originator of this type of test, as well as by others. But thus far it is the work of Mr. Forwald which stands out in this area, and it is work which presents some very challenging questions for future investigators of PK.

The emphasis in this chapter has been put largely on the question of evidence for the occurrence of PK. This is appropriate, because the establishment of a direct, extramuscular influence of thought upon physical systems has even greater revolutionary implications for psychology and biology than does the discovery of ESP. The general acceptance of the PK effect would require a reorientation of scientific thinking regarding the nature of the living organism—a reorientation in which the influence of mental factors would be recognized *in fact* and not in name only. But I need not dwell on the importance of the discovery that *thought processes have real force!*

But something should be said regarding the secondary problems—questions about the nature of PK—which have received some attention in the research. We have made a start toward finding out whether the PK effect is limited by the space and mass aspects of the physical situation. Thus far we have found no differences in relation to the number, mass, shape, and distance of the objects the subject was attempting to influence. Also, subjects have tried to influence a range of *types* of objects with apparent success, including dice and cubes, coins and other discs, spheres, roulette, a spinning pointer, the swimming of paramecia, and the growth of plants and molds. On these points the present results are inadequate for final conclusions, but the findings encourage further explorations in search of the scope and limits of PK in relation to the physical world.

Investigations bearing upon the psychology of PK have also shown some progress. Motivation appears to be a factor of paramount importance. Subjects who succeeded in their first series of tests have often failed in later efforts to demonstrate their PK abilities: the excitement and eager curiosity which marked their first experience could not be recaptured. Thus investigators have learned that success in a test for PK, as with ESP, is not to be taken for granted. In general, exact duplication of the results of experiments has been as difficult for PK as for ESP.

The findings of parapsychology form but a beachhead on a new continent of the world of science. The facts I have been presenting show that PK, like ESP, is a part of that beachhead. There are uncertainties in the situation but they are not concerned with the evidence for the *occurrence* of the phenomena. They relate, rather, to what we will find as we move on beyond the perimeter of our small beachhead of unshakable evidence and extend our lines of exploration and discovery. The uncertainties are merely the challenge to further research.

5

Mind on the Rampage?
The Seaford Poltergeist

The year 1958 began for me not unlike any number of others. I had recently accepted Dr. Rhine's suggestion that I should give up a project for the investigation of pigeon homing supported by a grant from the Office of Naval Research (see Chapter 9). Over a period of several years this work had involved me in field studies that kept me away from my desk a great deal of the time. To free myself from this pleasant duty, I transferred the pigeon-homing project to the Duke University Zoology Department, and I slipped quietly back into harness in the laboratory.

Then, early in February, a friend of the laboratory in the New York region sent us the first clipping about some household disturbances which had broken out in the James M. Herrmann home in Seaford, Long Island. These events involved the movement of household objects and other physical effects for which the observers who were on the scene could find no explanation. The mysterious occurrences appeared to center around the son, James, who was in early adolescence. Thus the disturbances fitted into the pattern of the typical "poltergeist" (mischievous spirit) of which there have been some hundreds of cases recorded throughout history. Several earlier cases had been investigated by experienced research workers with results that only made the mystery seem deeper and therefore more challenging and more worthy of continued study.

The newspaper clippings about the Long Island case continued to reach Dr. Rhine's desk over a period of several days. As the case developed, it seemed to be an especially promising one for scientific investigation. First in importance was the existence of a full and carefully compiled record of the developments in the form of an official police report. On February 11, eight days after the disturbances started, Detective Joseph Tozzi of the Nassau County Police was assigned to full-time duty on the case. From then until the final disturbance took place on March 10 (and for an indefinite period after that, since the case remained unsolved) he was on call twenty-four hours a day whenever any new outbreak occurred, and he carefully interviewed the people who were in the house at the time and recorded their accounts within a short period, usually only a few minutes after the disturbances happened.

Another advantage of this case from the point of view of scientific study is the fact that several people outside the family were in the house when some of the unexplained events took place.

Still another fortunate circumstance was the desire of

the family for help toward understanding the cause of their trouble and bringing it to an end. Consequently they gladly opened their doors to the investigators from the Parapsychology Laboratory at Duke (as to others who took an interest in the case) and willingly answered all questions put to them.

The disturbances appeared to be increasing in both number and magnitude. Especially, the stories that appeared in the Long Island paper, *Newsday*, gave an impression of intelligent observation and genuine puzzlement on the part of the reporter, Mr. David Kahn. These things added up to a decision by the laboratory to move in on the case.

The first contact was made through Mr. Kahn, who agreed that he would keep the laboratory's interest in the matter out of the news until the investigation had been completed, with the understanding that he would at that time get an exclusive story on our study of the disturbances. However, he had already imposed a great deal upon the family in covering the story, he felt somewhat responsible for what they had gone through as a result of the publicity, and he did not want to ask them to let him bring us in on the case as well.

Dr. Rhine had suggested that I should consider going up, so I placed a call to Mr. Herrmann. He appreciated our interest and said that the family would welcome my coming to help them get at the root of their difficulties.

A few hours later Mr. Kahn met me at La Guardia Airport. On the way to Seaford he said that his editor had vetoed the idea of keeping the investigation "off the record." The editor thought that this story was one of local interest only and that it had run its course. He intended, therefore, to wind up their coverage of it in the next morning's issue with a sort of "society news" item to the effect that the Parapsychology Laboratory of Duke University had sent me up to make a quiet study of the things that had been taking place in the Herrmann house. This did not seem like a correct appraisal of the situation to me, but the matter, as presented, seemed beyond my control.

We were met at the door by Mrs. Herrmann, who was obviously quite excited. She said that we should go down to the rumpus room in the basement and see what had happened only a short time before.

We did so, and there we found Sergeant McConnell, Detective Tozzi's superior on the Nassau County police force, looking at the wreckage of a small record player. This was on the floor in the corner of the room near the foot of the steps, diagonally across the room and approximately twenty feet from the place on the opposite wall where the phonograph ordinarily sat on a special metal table. Sergeant McConnell said the call that a new disturbance had taken place had come to the police station a short while before; and since Detective Tozzi was not immediately available, he had himself come to investigate.

He found that three members of the family were in the house when the phonograph was wrecked. The young son in the family, James (aged twelve), reported that he had been sitting at a study table which was in a nook under the stairway in the rumpus room, and he caught only a glimpse of a quick motion before he heard the crash of the record player as it struck the lower part of the staircase banister. Mrs. Herrmann and James's sister (aged thirteen) were both upstairs, and they only heard the noise. The metal table itself had turned over and the records which were on a lower, "V" shelf had spilled out onto the floor.

According to the rules which strictly governed the family after each new disturbance, nothing was touched. Sergeant McConnell had come as soon as he received Mrs. Herrmann's call.

Mr. Kahn, Sergeant McConnell, and I had been talking only a few minutes when Mr. Herrmann got home from the city. He showed consternation over what he saw, and he was vehemently outspoken in wanting to see an end put to these mysterious disturbances.

Mr. Herrmann soon joined the other members of the family on the main floor while Mr. Kahn, Sergeant Mc-Connell, and I remained for a time in the basement. Sergeant McConnell was speaking about the difficulties of really getting to the heart of the matter. The investigation was entirely novel for the Nassau County Police. They had long since satisfied themselves that there was no criminal violation of law involved; but once they had accepted the case, they felt compelled to pursue it as long as it remained unsolved. The Herrmanns were obviously being harassed in some unexplained way, and they were entitled to police protection. He went on to say that he had personally become convinced that the case was not likely to be solved by the method that had been used up to that time, the plan of calling the detective only after a new outbreak had taken place. Rather, he thought that around-the-clock surveillance of the household might be required.

As we talked, there occurred a rapid sound of running feet and loud voices on the floor above. Going up to see what the noise was all about, we found Mr. and Mrs. Herrmann in the master bedroom. Mrs. Herrmann had discovered that a lamp on her dresser just inside the door was turned over. Mr. Herrmann was asking who had been in the room and the information appeared to be that Mrs. Herrmann was the last one there and that she had only just left the room.

While we were talking in the master bedroom, the two children were in the opposite end of the house where Lucille was preparing dinner. James had already taken his seat at the table and started eating. Lucille came from the kitchen into the dining room with a plate containing pieces of bread. At that moment the doorbell rang, and she placed the bread on the table in front of James and went to answer the door. When Lucille came back into the dining room a few seconds later she found the bread plate lying on the floor in the corner of the room with the bread scattered about. James said that he had been looking down at his own plate and had not seen anything. The first he knew about what had happened was when he heard the plate hit the floor.

Such was the particular set of events which marked my own entry onto the stage of the drama that had been unfolding for the past twenty-two days in the Herrmann household. Nothing that had happened since my arrival justified, of course, any conclusion that anything beyond ordinary human means had been involved in these events. In fact, the presence of James alone in the rumpus room when the record player crashed and in the dining room alone when the bread plate took flight made possible a very obvious explanation, and I could not establish beyond question that no one had been in the master bedroom between the time Mrs. Herrmann had left it and when she returned later to discover the lamp upset.

Things had happened too fast immediately before and after my arrival, and I had not yet begun to get a "feel" of what I was facing. We talked on until bedtime, and then Mr. Kahn offered to take me to dinner and to help me locate a hotel somewhere in the neighborhood. Before leaving, I had an understanding with Mrs. Herrmann that I would call her the next day about noon. Nothing had ever happened while the children were at school, and there seemed no point in my coming to the house until just before they were expected home early in the afternoon.

Only Mr. Kahn and I knew where I was staying. For a few hours, therefore, I was completely lost as far as the Herrmann family was concerned.

The following forenoon I telephoned Dr. Rhine to report upon developments of the first day of my visit, as already described. We agreed that the events did not give us much to go on, but that these occurrences taken alone were consistent with a suspicion expressed by a rival newspaper on Long Island—one that had covered the story from a distance and with a more hardheaded, cynical point of view. It had been voicing the common-sense if not the obvious solution that Jimmy had been playing pranks. But in spite of that we agreed that it was worth while for me to stay long enough to go fully into the matter, and particularly to look into the past record of the case as it existed in the detective's report.

About noon I rang up Mrs. Herrmann as agreed. She immediately said, with a note of concern in her voice, that the house was full of reporters who had come out from New York. Knowing of our desire not to have any publicity until the investigation was completed, she wanted to know if she should try to send them away. I said that once the reporters were interested and actually on the scene there was nothing to do but to talk to them, and I would come over as planned.

The growth of popular interest in the case over the next few weeks showed how badly the *Newsday* editor had misjudged the situation. The local whirlwind of publicity which he thought was blowing itself out at the time I arrived turned into a storm which spread the news of the Seaford case around the world.

This turn of events was most unfortunate as far as the investigation itself was concerned. The popular writers and interviewers were impatient to know about my findings on the case before the investigation had been carried out. I could only state that our laboratory research on PK had given us a basis of renewed interest in these household disturbances. I had no conclusions and we were not optimistic about being able to reach any. Even more serious from the scientific point of view was the fact that the presence of so many strangers in the house completely changed the psychological atmosphere. As we would expect, under the circumstances the poltergeist activities ceased.

When it became apparent that the wave of publicity that had inundated the Herrmann house made it hopeless to continue the investigation there, I shifted my base of operations to the Nassau County Police Station where I spent my time studying the fifty-page dossier that Detective Tozzi had already built up on the case. When my hiding place was discovered after two days and the demands upon my time for statements about the case and our reasons for being interested in it showed no signs of letting up, it appeared that the only sensible thing to do was to leave. Having requested Mr. Herrmann to let me know immediately if the disturbances began again, I left on March 1 on another field investigation.

After three days I was back at Duke. There had been no telephone call, and we supposed that all was quiet on the Seaford front. Then, to our surprise, we read in the New York *Times* that there had been a particularly active new outbreak of the mysterious events in the Herrmann home. A second visit seemed in order if we could find some way to make it without attracting the notice of the reporters. We decided, also, that the situation called for sending two investigators from the laboratory and that Mr. William G. Roll, Jr., should go along this time if he would like to do so. He was glad to accept the invitation.

For the second visit, our approach was through Detective Tozzi. He agreed to keep the fact that we were coming secret, and he impressed upon the family that nothing was to be said about the visit. For a period of several days both Mr. Roll and I moved freely into and out of the Herrmann house without once encountering a reporter. A few times a writer came to the home when we were inside, but we went to the rumpus room and waited until the coast was clear. At this stage the reporters were telephoning to the house frequently to inquire whether anything further had happened, and the member of the family who answered the phone always said that nothing more had taken place. Indeed, the unexplained events *had* largely stopped, but during the time we were together in the home Mr. Roll and I did hear at one time a series of explosive sounds which we could not definitely explain; and on another occasion we heard a loud explosion which literally shook the house. This proved to be associated with definite physical disturbances which we were able to investigate, as will be described later in this chapter.

Other things needed for the completion of the record of the case were also done during this time. These activities included getting a complete copy of the official police record, conducting interviews with members of the family as well as with neighbors and relatives who had been involved with the case, and getting an accurate, scaled floor plan of the house. I finished my part of the work and left ahead of Mr. Roll, who stayed on alone for a few days under similar circumstances of quiet, uninterrupted investigation—the kind that we had expected to conduct from the beginning of our involvement in the case. In all, each of us spent ten days in Seaford, our two periods overlapping for six days.

The pages that follow give a detailed summary of our findings on the case as these were finally assembled and reported in the *Journal of Parapsychology* for June 1958. The amount of interest taken in the matter at the time appears to justify presenting the study in sufficient detail to show how carefully the mystery was probed from a great number of points of view in searching for some explanation in ordinary terms. Yet it is only fair to say at the outset that, in spite of the fact that no such solution was found, we did not feel that our investigation justified a definite conclusion regarding a parapsychological basis of the disturbances. This case comes within an unusual zone of problems even as viewed by the parapsychologist, and it would be a mistake to take the length of the present chapter as an indication that these strange occurrences have yielded anything definite to the general findings of the field. Yet they continue to hold a fascination for the research worker as they do for the general public, and the challenge is one that should not be ignored.

Sixty-seven distinct mysterious events were listed from the beginning of the disturbances on February 3 until the last one occurred on March 10. From the scientific point of view, not all of the events were of equal interest. The majority of them, in fact, could easily have been produced normally under the circumstances that existed, though there was never any direct evidence that anything was done deliberately as a prank or simply for effect. From the point of view of the study of the case, we should focus attention upon those happenings that make it most difficult to think of an ordinary explanation.

The first group of events of unusual interest consists of those instances in which objects were actually seen to start to move without contact. Four out of the sixty-seven disturbances were of this sort. The first such instance was a double event in that two objects were seen to move at the same time. The following is an excerpt from the police record concerning Sunday, February 9:

> Mr. Herrmann standing in bathroom doorway, son James at sink brushing teeth, actually saw a bottle of Kaopectate move along the formica top of the drain in a southerly direction for about 18″ and fall into the sink. At the same time a bottle of shampoo moved along the formica drain in a westerly direction and fell to the floor. There was no noise or vibration and no one touched either bottle to move them.

When Mr. Roll and I questioned Mr. Herrmann and James about these two events, their description was entirely consistent with that found in the police report. Our interviews and observations brought the following additional facts to light: Mrs. Herrmann had cleaned up the bathroom cabinet after the shampoo and the Kaopectate bottles had spilled a short time before, and she had placed these two bottles on the vanity table. Mr. Herrmann saw *both* bottles start to move. He said that James "froze" in his position. James said he saw the Kaopectate bottle when it fell into the sink. He did not see the other bottle, though of course he heard the crash as it hit the floor.

Mr. Herrmann stated that it was this occurrence which convinced him that the disturbances in his home were of an unusual character and led him immediately thereafter to lodge a complaint with the Nassau County Police Department. He wrote the following statement for us on March 14:

> At *about* 10:30 A.M. I was standing in the doorway of the bathroom. All of a sudden two bottles which had been placed on the top of the vanity table were seen to move. One moved straight ahead, slowly, while the second spun to the right for a 45° angle. The first one fell into the sink. The second one crashed to the floor. Both bottles moved at the same time.
>
> Both bottles had become unscrewed while they were in the cabinet under the sink. They had been placed on the vanity top while the cabinet was being cleaned.
>
> (Signed) *James M. Herrmann*

The vanity table on which the bottles stood is slightly tilted toward the sink and the floor. The tilt is about one sixteenth of an inch per foot. The top is made of formica. Mr. Roll tested the Kaopectate bottle by placing it on the top after having wet it with soapy water to minimize the friction. (Mr. Herrmann stated that the counter top was clean and dry when he saw the bottles move.) The bottle did not slide for Mr. Roll even when pushed. He then made a test with a small marble (about half an inch diameter) by placing it on the vanity top where the bottles had stood. It would not roll by itself, but if pushed slightly would continue rolling diagonally across the board, not directly toward the sink or edge.

Another occurrence in which an object was seen to move took place on Saturday, February 15, at 7:40 P.M. when only the two children and their adult second cousin, Miss Marie Murtha, were in the living room. The visitor left shortly after this event and before Detective Tozzi arrived. He therefore based his first report on interviews with the family, but contacted Miss Murtha two days later by telephone and obtained her firsthand account of this event. This is summarized in the police record as follows:

She stated that she is the cousin of Mr. Herrmann and was visiting at his home on Saturday, February 15, 1958, and stated that she was sitting in the living room of the complainant's home and the two children were with her. The boy was sitting in the center of the sofa and the girl was standing next to Miss Murtha, who was sitting in a chair in the northeast corner of the living room. Mrs. Herrmann went into the bathroom and when she turned on the light in there it caused interference on the television set. The girl started across the room to fix the set and before she got there the picture cleared by itself. The girl came back to where Miss Murtha was sitting and the boy was still sitting on the sofa with his arms folded. At this time a porcelain figurine that was standing on the end table at the south end of the sofa was seen to leave the table and fly through the air for about

two feet, directly at the television set. The figurine
fell to the floor about six inches from the television
with a loud noise. The figurine fell to the floor but
did not break. Miss Murtha stated that she actually
saw the occurrence and there was definitely no one in
the room that was close enough to touch the figurine
or propel it in any way.

On March 13 I had an interview with Miss Murtha,
a single, middle-aged lady, in her home in the Bronx,
New York. Her description was consistent with the account she had earlier given the police. Some of the details were amplified as follows.

When Lucille went to look at her hair in the glass
front of the secretary, James made some joking remark
to Miss Murtha about Lucille and her hair and Miss
Murtha turned to listen to him. When she did, she
noticed the female figurine on the end table begin to
move—"wiggle" was the word she used. Then, when she
was looking directly at the figurine, it left its position on
the end table very suddenly and moved through the air
in the direction of the TV so rapidly that she could not
really see it, but only saw something like a white streak
or white feather in rapid motion. She thought that the
figurine had turned and that it was its white back which
she saw. It landed with a very loud crash. She could not
tell whether it had struck the TV, the floor, or the rug.
There were no marks on the TV or floor, and the figurine ended its fall on the rug so it may have struck
there; but it made an unusually loud noise. The figurine
was not broken and she could not imagine why it was

not. Immediately afterward, Mr. Herrmann came into the living room from the central hallway entrance and asked who had knocked the figurine off the table. Miss Murtha said she told him that no one had done it, she had seen it start to move and then fly off by itself while James was sitting with his arms folded in the middle of the couch looking directly at her.

Miss Murtha impressed me as being levelheaded and intelligent. She said that her idea was that the things which had been happening in the house must have an electrical cause, and recalled an event from her childhood in which she had seen a coffeepot hurled to the ceiling when it caused a short circuit on an electrical heating unit. She could not explain the events in her cousin's home but she did not believe that anything supernatural was involved. She lamented the publicity and was afraid of its effect on the children.

As I left, I asked Miss Murtha if she would write a letter describing her experience in connection with the figurine. The relevant paragraph from this letter (dated March 17) is given below:

> James, his sister, Lucille, and myself were sitting in the living room—I was sitting in the green chair in the corner between the secretary and the window—James and Lucille were seated on the sofa—there is a table at each end of this sofa—on one table was a lighted lamp and two figurines—we were looking at the television when the picture started to flicker—I asked Lucille to adjust it—as she went to do so the picture cleared—on her way back to her seat I asked to feel

the material in her slacks and remarked that they were smart, but thought she was neglecting to set her hair. Lucille then turned to look at herself in the glass of the secretary and James said, "Auntie Marie, she is always fixing her hair"—I turned my head in his direction to answer him—as I did I saw the female figurine wiggle (like that of a worm cut in pieces)—as it went in the air it looked like a small white feather —then crashed to the rug, unbroken. The children's parents were in other rooms of the house and hearing the crash came hurrying into the living room to see what happened.

(Signed) *Marie H. Murtha*

The fourth and final event in which an object was seen to start to move involved a small night table. The police record contains the following statements about this event, which took place on Sunday, March 2:

On the above date at about 2210 hours [10:10 P.M.] James was in bed, as was Lucille. Mrs. Herrmann was in the kitchen and Mr. Herrmann was sitting in the easy chair in the southwest corner of the living room facing the boy's room. A very loud crash was heard and Mr. Herrmann ran immediately into the boy's room. As he got to the door of the boy's room a small three-drawer night table which had been about 18″ to the north of the bed twisted and fell to the floor across the door. The boy was on his back in bed with the covers up to his chin at the time the complainant got into the room. Apparently the first crash was the brass lamp on the top of the night table as it was on the floor and the base was badly bent as if the night table had fallen on it. The glass globe was broken but the bulb inside was not. Mr. Herrmann was almost in the doorway when the table fell and he had a flashlight in his hand. The light was on and he stated that the boy was lying in the bed and appeared very frightened. He did not move at all to the complainant's knowledge.

On the evening of Friday, March 7, 1958, Mr. Herrmann, discussing the occurrences of the last few days with Mr. Roll and myself, stated that before the event of the previous Sunday evening involving the end table had taken place, he had felt that something more would happen that night. Accordingly, he took his position in the chair in the southeast corner of the living room facing toward the hallway and looking into the boy's darkened bedroom. His flashlight in his hand, he was prepared to spring toward James's room immediately if any sound came. When there was a noise, he dashed into the room with the flashlight burning, and snapped on the ceiling light in the room. He stated that he saw the boy lying quietly in bed and that, before his eyes, the end table turned about ninety degrees and then fell forward onto the floor without any visible means to account for the motion.

A second class of disturbances which are relevant to the question of whether any of the events were parapsychological or psychokinetic in nature are mysterious events which took place when no one was near. These are happenings in which the exact location of the persons in the house, as clearly indicated by corroborated testimony, makes it highly unlikely that any of them could have produced the disturbances in any ordinary way without discovery. There are thirteen occurrences of this kind.

The first event recorded as having taken place when no one was in a position to have done it normally was a bottle that jumped from a cardboard box in the unfinished part of the cellar on February 3. The police record has the following statement concerning this occurrence:

> Mrs. Herrmann and Jim, Jr., in the cellar actually saw a half-gallon bottle of Clorox leave a cardboard box and fall to the floor and break. Mrs. Herrmann and James were about six feet away from the box at this time.

When interviewed by the writers, Mrs. Herrmann and James both said that they had not actually seen the bottle leave the box. Mrs. Herrmann said that the first thing she was aware of was the crash when the bottle struck the floor in front of her when they were about halfway across the room. James stated that he saw the bottle just before it hit the floor, and he automatically pulled some clothes, on the lines that crossed the middle of the room, in front of his mother to protect her from flying glass and splashing liquid.

The next disturbances in this category were a closely grouped series of bottle poppings in the master bedroom, kitchen, bathroom, and cellar. The explosive noises were heard by the members of the family, all of whom were together in the dining room at the time. These disturbances took place on Sunday, February 9, and they are described as follows in the police record:

At about 1015 hours [10:15 A.M.] the whole family was in the dining room of the house. Noises were heard to come from different rooms and on checking, it was found that a holy water bottle on the dresser in the master bedroom had opened and spilled, a new bottle of toilet water on the other dresser in the master bedroom had fallen, lost its screw cap and also a rubber stopper, and the contents were spilled. At the same time, a bottle of shampoo and a bottle of Kaopectate in the bathroom had lost the caps and fallen over and were spilling their contents. The starch in the kitchen was also opened and spilled again and a can of paint thinner in the cellar had opened, fallen, and was spilling on the floor.

After this outbreak of weird explosions, the police were called in for the first time, and a short time later the noise of a bottle overturning in the bathroom was heard when Patrolman Hughes and the entire family were in the living room. The statement from the police record concerning this particular event on Sunday, February 9, is as follows:

While Patrolman J. Hughes was at the complainant's home all the family was present with him in the living room when noises were heard in the bathroom. When Patrolman Hughes went into the bathroom with the complainant's family he found the medicine and shampoo had again spilled.

On March 10, Mr. Roll and I had an interview with Patrolman Hughes. He stated that a single bottle was involved in the incident which happened while he was in the house. When he and the whole family were in the living room they heard a noise from the bathroom as if a bottle had fallen over. When the bathroom was inspected, a bottle on the vanity table was found on its side.

Hughes had inspected the bathroom prior to this occurrence. It had at that time already been cleaned up after the last disturbance (when Mr. Herrmann had seen the two bottles move in different directions) and he was convinced that the bottle was not then lying down ("I can swear to that!"). When further questioned, Hughes said he could not exclude the possibility that someone had turned the bottle over after he had first seen the bathroom, but in this event he could not account for the noise.

A more striking event which took place when no one was nearby was the crash of a figurine in the living room when Mrs. Herrmann and both children were together in the hallway seeking to escape flying objects. This event is one of a number of disturbances which took place during the evening of Thursday, February 20. The immediately preceding occurrence finally led Mrs. Herrmann to take the children with her into the hallway, the only part of the house that had been free of disturbances. The previous occurrences and the one involving the figurine are described as follows in the police record:

On the above date at about 2145 hours [9:45 P.M.] Mrs. Herrmann was on the phone in the dining room,

James was right next to her and Lucille was in the bedroom. James was putting his books away and there was a bottle of ink on the south side of the table. A very loud pop was heard and the ink bottle lost its screw top and the bottle left the table in a north-easterly direction. The bottle landed in the living room and the ink spilled on the chair, floor and on the wallpaper on the north side of the front door. Mrs. Herrmann immediately hung up and called the writer, who had left the house about 10 minutes prior to this occurrence. When the writer arrived it was learned that as soon as Mrs. Herrmann called, she had taken the two children with her into the hallway to await the arrival of the writer. At about 2150 hours [9:50 P.M.] while the children were with her a loud noise was again heard in the living room. All three of them went into the room and found the figurine had again left the end table and had again flown through the air for about 10 feet and again hit the desk about six inches to the east of where it had hit the first time. On this occurrence the only noise heard was when the figurine hit the desk and at this time it broke into many pieces and fell to the floor. At this time the only appliance running was the oil burner and no one was again in the room.

We questioned each of the three people separately on their movements during this period. The facts were corroborated as reported. The three were standing in the end of the hall near the bathroom out of sight of the living room when the loud crash sounded. Mrs. Herrmann was standing with her back to the linen closet and James and Lucille were standing in front of the bathroom door. They were all facing one another.

Another major item was the overturning of the dresser in James's bedroom when it seems clear that the room was empty. This event took place on Monday, February 24, and it is described in the police record as follows:

> On the above date at about 1640 hours [4:40 P.M.] the complainant was in the kitchen fixing dinner. Dave Kahn and Mr. Herrmann were in the dining room, both children were in the cellar, when a loud crash was heard from the boy's room. All ran to the room and found the dresser had again fallen over in a southerly direction. At the time of occurrence James, Jr., was coming up the cellar stairs and Lucille was sitting at the table in the cellar. When the complainant, Kahn, and Mr. Herrmann got into the hall the boy was just coming up the stairs. The cellar door was closed at the time.

During my first visit I questioned all the members of the family and found that they individually agreed with the description given in the police report. Mr. Kahn was interviewed on March 15 by Mr. Roll and the following notes, which had been made immediately after the occurrence, were obtained:

> February 24, Mon. at 4:40 P.M. while Jim [Mr. Herrmann] and I in dinette going over phone calls about the matter, a loud rumble and crash—scary again—and both of us realized that it was another object going over—jumped up and ran to Jimmy's room—he at doorway after coming up from downstairs where he was working on his stamp collection— Lucille in cellar: "It sounded like the walls were caving in, I thought it came from the living room, the

dining room, everywhere." Mrs. H. in kitchen fixing dinner. DK toilet articles [which Kahn had left on James's dresser], including bottle of hair tonic, went over and bottle broke.

From the wording of the police report this event sounded as if it might be an instance in which the occurrence of a major disturbance in an empty room could be vouched for by someone other than a member of the family. Mr. Roll, in his interview with Mr. Kahn, asked him whether he could testify that James was in the cellar at the time the bureau turned over. Mr. Kahn replied that he could not so state; by the time he reached the hallway, James was standing in the hall looking through the open doorway into his bedroom. The report given by James and corroborated by Lucille is that both of them had been seated at the table, back of the stairway in the rumpus room, and that James had just left his chair. James said he had to go to the bathroom. Both children said he was only part way up the stairway when a loud noise described as a rumbling sound seemed to come from all over the house. For a short time James stopped on the stairway, then he proceeded to the head of the stairs and was on the point of opening the door when his father rushed from the dining room into the hallway. Since the door to the cellar stair blocks the hallway when open, James waited until his father had passed. He then followed his father to the bedroom doorway, where he was standing when Mr. Kahn reached the hallway.

When questioned regarding the apparent discrepancy

between the official record and Mr. Kahn's statement, Mr. Herrmann said that when the noise occurred he leaped from his chair so quickly that he turned it over and he did not take time to catch it. He stated that Mr. Kahn, being less accustomed to the disturbances, was startled and did not react so quickly. Mr. Kahn took longer to reach the central hallway where he could see past the cellar door. Thus the statement that James was on the cellar stairway when the bureau overturned in his room rests on the testimony of Mr. Herrmann and of Lucille.

Again, there was on another occasion a crash which appeared from the record and from our subsequent investigation to have taken place in an empty room. This involved a figure of the Virgin Mary in the master bedroom. The police record describes this event, which took place on Tuesday, February 25, in the following words:

At about 0720 [7:20 A.M.], this date the complainant was in the kitchen, Mr. Herrmann had gone to work, and both children were in their rooms getting dressed for school. A loud crash was heard and Mrs. Herrmann ran immediately to the hall. She asked what had happened and both children stated it wasn't in their rooms. All of them went into the master bedroom and found that a 16″ plaster figure of the Virgin Mary had gone from Mr. Herrmann's dresser on the west wall to Mrs. Herrmann's dresser on the east wall. This figurine had knocked down Mrs. Herrmann's picture on Mr. Herrmann's dresser and had struck a wooden mirror frame over Mrs. Herrmann's dresser. The figurine then fell to the dresser and one hand broke off it. It also knocked down a lamp on the latter dresser and broke the bulb. All persons present stated that they had heard nothing prior to the crash and had not been in the master bedroom at the time of the occurrence.

On Thursday, February 27, Mrs. Herrmann discussed this case with me in the light of the implication given by one newspaper that James could have caused all the occurrences. She said that the children had been specifically instructed not to move from where they were when some disturbance occurred. When the noise in this instance was heard, James immediately called out from his room that it was not in there. Thus he confirmed the fact that he was not in the master bedroom at the time of the impact. For the damage to have been done as it was, James would have had to throw the figure from a position directly in front of the mirror which was struck in the master bedroom. If he called out at once from his own room, he would not have had time to get there before identifying his position.

Could James have staged the occurrence, upsetting his mother's picture on his father's bureau and then throwing the figure from the hallway near his own bedroom door? Under these conditions the figure could not have dented the *front and inside* surfaces of the mirror frame, neither would it have marred the bureau top directly below the point of impact on the mirror, or have fallen onto the floor in the spot where it was found. The overturned picture, the marks on the mirror, and the other effects are consistent with the interpretation that the object came from its customary position on Mr. Herrmann's bureau.

There were two other events when the positions of the members of the family and visitors were accounted for. Since they took place when Mr. Roll and I were in the house, they belong in the category of unexplained happenings that took place while I alone from the Duke laboratory was in the house or when both Mr. Roll and myself were present. The prospect of making a fully satisfactory study of such a case depends primarily upon whether the investigator is on the scene when disturbances are taking place. Five events among the total of sixty-seven recorded were of this sort, though they were not otherwise so striking as many of the other things that were reported as happening. Yet because they are what happened while one or both of us were there, they deserve to be listed separately in full.

The overturning of the lamp in the master bedroom and the fall of the bread plate from the dining table on the day I first arrived in Seaford have already been described earlier in this chapter. The upsetting of the lamp was one of the events which apparently took place when no one was near.

The bread-plate incident is of no value as evidence of anything beyond the ordinary, since James was sitting at the dining table alone when it happened, but a few comments on this event beyond what was said earlier may be worth while. I asked James if he had seen the plate move, and he answered that he had not; he was looking at his own plate and had not seen any motion—he had only heard the noise when the plate hit the floor. It would have been very easy for James to shove the bread off the table. But if he had done so, it is hard to imagine why he would have said that he did not see it move (which, in view of the fact that the plate was sitting only slightly toward his left, not more than four feet away from his eyes, is rather surprising). Would he not have got more out of his "prank" by saying that he saw the plate take off and sail through the air? This would have been more dramatic and at the same time easier to believe than the statement he made. However, this event by itself has no value as evidence of any parapsychological force.

After supper on March 9, I was watching TV with the children in the living room while Mr. Roll and Mr. Herrmann talked in the dining room. About 9:00 P.M. the children went to bed. At nine-forty James was in bed with the light out and the door open. Mrs. Herrmann was in the kitchen and Lucille was in her room in bed. At that time there was a dull thump, which I heard as coming from across the hall in the direction of the boy's room. Mrs. Herrmann came out of the kitchen into the hall toward James's room, asking: "What was that noise? Did anyone hear it?" I said yes and we both looked about in the bedrooms but found nothing. Then Mrs. Herrmann and Mr. Roll went to the basement, but nothing was found disturbed. Neither Mr. Roll nor Mr. Herrmann, who were talking in the dining room, had noticed the noise.

At nine forty-five there came another thump, louder than before, and all adults joined in the search. Mrs. Herrmann was obviously shaken. Lucille, still in bed, said it came from James's wall just as if he had hit it with his fist or elbow. I asked James to do this and he was able to get nearly the same sound. James said he was half awake both times the thumping noise was heard. These sounds are, of course, trivial in comparison with the other events and they would not be worth pointing out except for the sake of completing the record of what happened in the house while we were there.

The final one of the sixty-seven recorded disturbances happened on March 10 when Mr. Roll and I were both in the house. We were able to make a close study of this event, which involved the explosive removal of a metal screw-top cap from a bleach bottle in the basement when all the persons in the house were on the first floor. The details of the event itself and the nature and results of the investigation bear relating in full.

On the March evening in question, Mr. Herrmann stayed in New York to appear on a radio program. At 8:14 P.M. when Mr. Roll was sitting at the east end of the dining-room table and I was in the living room, there was a loud dull noise which to Mr. Roll sounded as if it came from the floor or lower wall of the kitchen-bathroom area. James was at that time in the bathroom, Lucille was in bed, and Mrs. Herrmann was in the master bedroom coming toward the central hallway. Mr. Roll investigated upstairs and I went down to the unfinished part of the cellar. Here I found that the bleach bottle in the cardboard box by the washing machine was standing on an overturned jar containing starch, and the bleach bottle had lost its cap and was leaning against the side of the box. The cap was on the floor back of the box. The contents of the bottle had not spilled, as it was not full.

At 8:30 P.M., sixteen minutes after the noise was heard,

we made an investigation of the cap of the bottle, which had fallen right side up. We found it to be still wet inside and there was a wet spot on the floor below the cap. We observed the wet spot thereafter at fifteen-minute intervals and we found that it had completely dried up within forty-five minutes of the time the noise was heard.

Though this event was of a minor sort as compared to some of the other disturbances, we were primarily concerned to see if it could be conclusively proved that this occurrence took place at the same time the noise was heard, as we knew the cellar was empty at the time.

This was important because the noise itself was not sufficiently well localized to establish definitely that it had come from the unfinished cellar rather than from the bathroom where James was at that time. Therefore we had to consider the possibility that he had some time earlier staged the bottle effect and then later produced the sound. We could definitely establish that James could not have been in the cellar during the thirty-minute period before the disturbance of the bleach bottle was discovered. For at least half an hour prior to the occurrence Mr. Roll was with James in the dining room where they were participating in a PK game with dice. When this ended shortly after 8:00 P.M. James went immediately to his room and then into the bathroom.

It was therefore important to find out whether the wet spot under the bottle cap could help to determine the time of the occurrence. Detective Tozzi and I observed later the same night that when a drop has formed on the inside of the cap, it comes off only if the cap is placed down forcefully and not if it is simply placed on the floor. Further tests that night and the next day by Mr. Roll and myself with the bleaching liquid showed that a spot of moisture on the concrete floor under the bottle cap will be visible for about three quarters of an hour, but moist and dark for only the first fifteen minutes or so. The spot discovered under the cap the night before sixteen minutes after the noise was heard was definitely dark in color.

If James had staged the event thirty minutes before he made the noise, which was forty-six minutes before the investigators observed the floor under the cap, the place where the cap was found should have been completely dry or the spot should have been only damp and on the point of fading away. In addition to this, it seems unlikely that there should be any spot at all if the events were staged, as a drop would become disengaged from the cap only if this was dropped from above or smartly tapped on the concrete.

The sound connected with the bleach bottle was similar in tonal quality to the two sounds (not associated with any discoverable physical disturbance) heard on the preceding evening. However, it was considerably louder than either of the previous thumps had been, and everyone in the house at the time heard the sound quite distinctly. Mr. Roll localized it as coming from low down in the region of the wall separating the kitchen from the bathroom, and James, when questioned by Mrs. Herrmann, said that he had not done anything in the bathroom that could have caused it.

On Thursday, March 13, Mr. Roll sat in the chair he

had occupied in the dining room when he heard the sound on the preceding Monday. I went to the unfinished cellar and struck several objects near the point where the bleach bottle was disturbed. Mr. Roll stated that the sounds I produced were "right" in so far as the localization was concerned, but not of the same quality as the one he had heard on Monday evening. I agreed that the tonal quality was not the same.

In our report, Mr. Roll and I considered whether the disturbances as a whole might be explained in some ordinary way, without invoking a parapsychological explanation. First, we discussed the possibility that one or both of the children caused the disturbances fraudulently (the "childish pranks hypothesis") and then whether Mr. and Mrs. Herrmann might have been party to a fraud (the "family hoax hypothesis").

The hypothesis of childish pranks was in our minds when we started the investigation and it was given serious consideration by the police in their work on the case as well as by the parents. On February 12, the day after Detective Tozzi came on the case, both children were interviewed by him. On being questioned, they denied they had anything to do with the occurrences. Detective Tozzi warned them that it would be a grave matter if they were found to be implicated in any way. The phenomena nevertheless continued, some of them even taking place when the detective was close by. On one of these occasions, when Detective Tozzi and James were alone in the cellar and a small metal horse fell to the floor close to the detective's feet, Mr. Tozzi immediately accused James, even (falsely) saying that he had seen the boy throw the horse. He subjected James to a long and severe grilling, the boy all the time denying that he had anything to do with this or any of the other incidents. During the afternoon and evening of Sunday, March 2, there were several disturbances. Before the arrival of Detective Tozzi that night, Mr. Herrmann, as he told Mr. Roll and me later, had vigorously accused James, saying that the detective had proof that James had caused many of the events and that it was time for him to admit it without further delay. The father said that James, driven to tears, only said, "Dad, I had nothing to do with any of it." (Mrs. Herrmann, who was present when Mr. Herrmann told us about this, said she did not approve the way her husband treated the boy on this occasion.) When Detective Tozzi arrived on the scene, "James was sitting at the dining-room table crying, Lucille was in the kitchen crying, and Mr. Herrmann was trying to bring some order to the house, as the complainant [Mrs. Herrmann] was also crying and on the verge of hysteria. At this time, the complainant and the two children went to the Liguoris' home to spend the night as they were afraid to sleep in their home. . . ."

The mysterious events clearly centered around James rather than Lucille (or any other member of the family). If the incidents were fraudulently produced, he would be the most likely culprit. James is an intelligent and likable boy. He seemed also to be frank and honest. However, let us assume that this exterior covered a hardened core which enabled him to stand up to the questioning by the detective and his father while continuing his destructive activities. Let us also assume the existence of some abnormality which made him direct these activities against his own possessions as well as those of his parents. James's or Lucille's possible complicity cannot be ruled out in a number of instances. These consist of several disturbances which occurred when they were alone in the house; a larger number when James was alone in the room in which the occurrences took place; and a miscellaneous assortment of effects which he alone or he and Lucille together *could* have produced.

But the important question is whether there were any disturbances that are difficult to place in the category of possible pranks, or any which cannot be so set aside. In the "difficult pranks" group are the occurrences which happened while a third person was actually observing the object that had been disturbed and when the location of James or Lucille was such that apparently neither could have been in bodily contact with this object. However, even some of these phenomena, on close investigation, reveal an opportunity for fraud which an audacious trickster might have taken advantage of—of course with very great risks of being found out. Such are the events that took place when some other person was in the room with James when the incident occurred. In this group, also, belong the cases when James was known to be in another room prior to and after a disturbance but when he could conceivably have brought the event about without detection by moving noiselessly and rapidly up to the object in question, upsetting it, and then returning to his former location.

However, seventeen out of the total of sixty-seven events carefully studied and recorded cannot, if correctly reported, be explained as easily performed, simple pranks. In each of these cases the position of the children at the time of the disturbance was known to some other person to be such that they definitely could not have thrown, pushed, or upset the object in question. In some of the cases, James was actually observed at the time of the occurrence and the object itself was seen when its movement began.

Is it conceivable that those disturbances which cannot be attributed to ordinary prankishness might have been produced by means of skilled magic? We ascertained that the performance of magic is not known to be among James's hobbies, and it is improbable that a boy would be interested in magic without having the fact become known. But on the remote assumption that James might have learned magic in secret, could he have produced in this way the effects which are not explainable as unskilled tricks?

The occurrences can be divided into two categories: the "bottle poppings" and the displacements of furniture and household objects. It has been proposed that the former might involve the application of some chemical knowledge and the latter, mechanical skills utilizing undetected devices. I will discuss the two categories of events in the light of these suggestions.

There were twenty-three recorded events involving the more or less explosive opening of screw-top bottles. It had been suggested that the effects observed in the opening of the bottles when no one was present were not beyond the skills acquired in science-club chemistry. The implication was that the bottles could have been opened by pressure generated chemically or physically in a way that left no trace and therefore was not detectable in the subsequent analysis made in some instances in the police laboratory. Whether a hypothesis of this sort is justified seemed to Mr. Roll and myself a point worthy of investigation, and we accordingly tested the effect of generating pressure inside screw-top bottles by converting carbon dioxide from its solid state ("dry ice") to gas. We discovered that when the top was left loose the pressure simply escaped with a low, hissing noise but without removing the cap. When the cap was screwed on as tightly as possible by hand, the pressure increased until it forced its way out around the threads but without perceptibly loosening the cap. When we tightened the cover mechanically, we were successful in exploding a bottle of relatively thin glass, but the cap remained on the broken top of the bottle. Such an effect was never observed in connection with the bottles that lost their caps in the Herrmann household. When we used a Clorox bottle of thick glass, even tightening the cover mechanically produced neither an explosion nor perceptible unscrewing. When the pressure built up sufficiently, the gas escaped around the cap. (Millions of housewives who have done pressure canning in glass jars know that pressure escapes from firmly closed lids without any loosening of the caps.) It is evident, of course, that with a different method of sealing an explosion could be made to occur. But the point is that pressure does not cause the tops to unscrew and come completely off, and this is true whether they are put on loosely, firmly by hand, or with mechanical force.

We found that it made no difference if the threads were well lubricated with machine oil.

Let us now turn to a consideration of the "skilled magic" theory in relation to some of the incidents I described earlier involving the movement of objects. Every one of these occurrences could have been brought about by mechanical devices. The question is whether the installation and operation of such devices could have remained undetected. It is conceivable that James might have caused a Clorox bottle to jump out of its box and break on the floor, as happened in one instance, by pulling a string tied to the bottle and hooked over a clothesline or nail in the ceiling. Some of the other disturbances are not so easy to account for in this way. For instance, it is very difficult to imagine how James could have caused the two bottles to move in opposite directions by threads or some other device when his father was standing close by watching him. And how he could have made the figurine fly off the end table when Miss Murtha was in the room looking at him.

Also, can anyone please explain how, by means of strings or an easily concealed device, James could have caused a sixteen-inch statue of the Virgin Mary to hit the dresser in the master bedroom in the way it did while he was in another room and how he could have caused the figurine to fly across the living room when he was in the hallway with his mother and sister? In these three figurine cases we also have to explain how the magical device could have generated the speed or force displayed. The figurine Miss Murtha saw moved so rapidly that it appeared as a "small white feather." The Virgin Mary statue left deep marks on the mirror frame, and one of the other figurines heavily scarred the secretary when it shattered against it.

To get an estimate of the force involved in this last figurine smashing, we hurled crockery against wood comparable to that of which the secretary was made. We had to use all our strength to produce similar indentations. It is difficult to conceive of how James could have installed an undiscovered device to propel the figurine horizontally with such force when he was not in the room. Detective Tozzi reached the front door immediately after this occurrence, so there was little chance to conceal a device before he arrived on the scene. It is as difficult to see how James could have installed the mechanism in the first place. The same figurine had flown against the secretary earlier in the evening, at seven fifty-five when Mr. Tozzi was in the basement. The detective replaced it on the end table and remained in the living room until about nine-thirty. James was sitting at the dining-room table during this time doing his homework. James is reported to have remained in the dining room until nine forty-five, when the family sought shelter in the hallway. It would therefore seem that he had no opportunity to prepare the complicated mechanism necessary to crash the figurine the second time. Similarly, with regard to the other incidents, the opportunity for James (or anyone else) to prepare a trick using a hidden device which would then have to be concealed was limited or non-existent.

The fraud hypothesis would become easier to accept if we could suppose that the other members of the family were acting as James's accomplices. We could then simply assume that the disturbances reported by the Herrmanns, such as the simultaneous movement of the two bottles in different directions, never occurred and that the various effects which the police and others observed had been staged. This leaves only those occurrences to be explained which took place while Patrolman Hughes, Miss Murtha, and the writer and Mr. Roll (the bleach-bottle incident) were in the house. But, unless Miss Murtha is disqualified for being a relative of the Herrmanns, these three events seem as difficult to explain as part of a colossal family joke on the world as they were on the supposition that James alone contrived them himself by magical devices.

There are other considerations which make the family-hoax explanation an unsatisfactory one. The Herrmanns would seem to have been inviting unnecessary trouble and running grave risks by asking the police and other investigators into their home and then staging the disturbances right under the noses of these visitors. A member of the Seventh Precinct force was in the house at the time six of the disturbances took place, but the police investigations and interviews failed to reveal anything suspicious. Similarly, no reporter or other visitor present when events took place uncovered any evidence that any of the disturbances had been fraudulently produced.

The police did not use fingerprinting methods in this investigation. They considered it would not have been possible to establish guilt within the family by this method since the objects disturbed were in constant use.

However, on February 19, five previously disturbed bottles, whose contents had been analyzed at the police laboratory, were dusted with fluorescent powder without the knowledge of anyone outside the police department and replaced in the original positions. Detective Tozzi told the family that he wanted to see if anything would again happen to these bottles, and he instructed each person not to touch them. He thereafter carried in his car a special lamp by means of which the fluorescent powder could be detected on the hands of any member of the family, but none of these bottles ever spilled again.

The educational background of the parents, their professions, and the position of the family in the community reveal no motive for a joint hoax. Mrs. Herrmann, aged thirty-eight at that time, was a registered nurse who held a supervisory position in a large hospital until the time of her marriage. Mr. Herrmann, aged forty-three, is an alumnus of Fordham University, and the interlines representative of Air France in New York City. He saw action in the Pacific during World War II as a sergeant in the Marine Corps and is a member of the Auxiliary Police of Seaford. Scores of people became closely acquainted with the members of the family during and after the disturbances, including Mr. Robert Wallace (the writer of an article in *Life*), Mr. Edward R. Murrow (who did a "Person-to-Person" program on the family), Father Graham (editor of the Catholic magazine, *America*), Mr. Irve Tunick (who wrote the script for the Armstrong Circle Theater program), and, of course, Mr. David Kahn, Mr. Joseph Tozzi, and Mr. Roll and myself. No one ever expressed publicly or to me privately any doubt about the sincerity and honesty of the members of the family.

The family seemed greatly upset by the destruction of their belongings. They also expressed concern that the disturbances might cause injury to someone. In fact, they moved to the homes of neighbors and relatives on four occasions, staying away from their own house for a total of six nights during the period of the disturbances.

Some of the incidents involved religious objects (the statue of the Virgin Mary and the holy-water bottles). Willful destruction and interference with these objects would amount to desecration and would constitute a serious religious offense. It seems unlikely that a family as devout as the Herrmanns would be party to such sacrilege.

On March 6, when the coffee table, a new and prized possession, turned upside down and was damaged, Detective Tozzi and Sergeant Reddy found Mrs. Herrmann "very upset over the occurrence. The complainant was crying the whole time interviewed by the writer [Detective Tozzi] and stated that she is ready to try anything to stop this disturbance. She doesn't believe in any supernatural powers but stated that 'if this is not stopped she will even be ready to try a medium spiritualist.'" Later that day Detective Tozzi called the rectory of the Church of St. William the Abbot with the request that the bishop be asked if it was possible to have the rite of exorcism carried out.

This was not a laboratory case, and it is not possible to come to the kind of conclusion which we can reach from a piece of research conducted under rigidly controlled conditions. However, the material on hand does allow us to state that the fraud hypothesis is not supported by the evidence collected by the police, the writer, and other observers. No clues have been found to indicate either simple or skilled trickery, and some of the events which took place in the Herrmann home cannot be so explained even assuming that the necessary skills and motives for trickery existed. But, as far as can be determined, there were no motives for a family hoax and no evidence that James possessed the skills to carry out some of the complex occurrences.

Group hallucinations might explain the few noises not associated with physical effects, but not the disturbances of objects. Were these latter, then, produced in some brief abnormal state of mind which came upon everyone while the objects were being knocked or thrown about and which no one was able to remember afterward? Such a hypothesis would rest on a purely speculative basis, for there is nothing in the history of abnormal psychology to suggest that the four members of a family could simultaneously undergo such sudden and complete shifts in personality. Furthermore, the police and other visitors, including the writer, would have had to fall under the spell, perhaps even help in the staging of the incident. In my judgment, the "psychological aberration hypothesis" did not at the time merit, and has not at any time since merited, serious consideration.

Throughout their investigation the police hoped to find a physical cause underlying the disturbances and to bring them to an end by removing this cause. Detective Tozzi, together with his superiors and colleagues, went to considerable effort in the attempt to unearth a physical cause. Some of the investigations and consultations which had this aim are briefly described below.

The police first thought that the disturbances might be due to high-frequency radio waves. A person with a radio transmitter license living close by was interviewed on February 11, but was found not to have used his set for several years.

The Long Island Lighting Company was then contacted and on February 13 installed an oscillograph in the cellar where it was left for one day. It was placed there again on March 7 and remained in the cellar until the end of the disturbances. No unusual vibrations were associated with the three occurrences which took place during this period. The last of these was the bleach-bottle event in the same room as the oscillograph.

On February 13, five of the bottles which had lost their caps and spilled part of the contents were taken to the police laboratory in Mineola. They were found to contain no foreign matter.

The Long Island Lighting Company returned on February 17 to check the wiring, fuse panels, and ground wires. Everything was found to be in order.

On February 20, Detective Tozzi checked all outlets and turned the TV and oil burner on and off to see if they were connected with the occurrences. He also checked fuse boxes, water leaders, ground connections, and electrical insulations in the attic and elsewhere.

The next day a Mrs. Connolly phoned Tozzi, saying that there had been similar occurrences in her house which stopped when a chimney cap was installed to exclude downdrafts. After consultation with the building inspector of Hempstead and several others, Detective Tozzi arranged for Mr. Herrmann to purchase a turbine chimney cap and this was installed.

An electrician checked the house wiring on February 22 for possible vibrations.

On February 24, Detective Tozzi asked a Catholic priest, who is also an engineer, whether in his opinion there might be a physical cause not yet investigated. He did not think so and said the disturbances might be caused by other than natural means. (An inquiry was also made about the rites of exorcism and it was learned that permission must be given by a bishop. Detective Tozzi was told that exorcism is generally used only when church property is desecrated. Moreover, the rite is generally used on one person who is allegedly possessed of evil and not in a case of this kind.)

On the same day Detective Tozzi and Mr. Herrmann removed the storm windows in the cellar on the possibility that there was not enough circulation of air in the house.

The Seaford Fire Department checked a well in front of the house on February 25. They found that there had been no radical change in the water level in the past five years.

On February 26, maps were received from the Town of Hempstead Engineers Office showing this area before the house had been built. No water or streams were shown.

On the same day, an RCA test truck and crew tested

for radio frequencies outside the house. Nothing unusual was discovered.

An inspection was also made by the Town of Hempstead Building Department which found the house to be structurally sound, showing only normal settling cracks in the basement floor.

On February 28, a conference was held at Adelphi College with members of the science departments by Captain Lada, Sergeant Reddy, and Detective Tozzi for any ideas on the disturbances. No suggestions were offered.

A professor of engineering from Cooper Union, as well as a structural engineer, a civil engineer, and an electrical engineer from the Nassau County Society of Professional Engineers visited the police station and the Herrmann home on March 1 to try to determine the cause of the disturbances. Their examination of the house did not reveal anything.

On March 3, Mitchel Field was contacted for a list of planes leaving on the runway facing the Herrmann house and for their departure times. This information was obtained on March 5, but no correlations were found between the disturbances and checking times or flight directions.

The TV antenna was removed from the chimney on March 4 and a small crack was closed between the concrete foundation and the main base of the house to eliminate possible vibrations.

On March 5 the plumbing was checked and a slight vibration was detected from the circulator when this was running. The vibration was carried by a hot-water main to one of the main beams. However, one of the neighboring houses was checked for comparison and the vibrations there were found to be much greater.

Even without these investigations and consultations involving professional physicists and engineers, one could have safely concluded that the causes underlying these disturbances were not explainable as due to energy acting without some guiding intelligence. The selection of objects was too precisely localized for such causes as drafts of air, vibrations, magnetic forces, etc., to have brought about the disturbances. For instance, how are we to account for the fact that one figurine flew from an end table while another only a few inches away was left undisturbed? How, again, can the opening of bottles with screw caps be explained in purely physical terms?

Instead of evidence pointing to some undiscovered physical causes, the disturbances contained several clues indicating their *psychological* origin.

Nothing ever happened while all the family were out of the house, when they were fast asleep, or while the children were both at school. With the possible exception of one case, James was known to be in the house during all the disturbances. Other members of the family were frequently absent. Also, the disturbances took place nearer to James, on the average, than to any other member of the family.

The occurrences were not randomly scattered throughout the house. Also some sort of pattern can be discerned in the kinds of objects that were disturbed.

Moreover, the Seaford phenomena show a striking conformity to the general pattern established by earlier such cases, of which nearly five hundred have been studied sufficiently to be recorded in the serious literature dealing with such matters. In most of them, as in the Seaford case, unusual noises and unexplained happenings are centered around someone near the age of adolescence. At the same time this case, as is also the rule with many other such occurrences, had its own distinctive characteristics, the most pronounced of which is the "bottle poppings," when screw-top bottles lost their caps with a loud noise, turned over, and spilled their contents.

The indications from these many features of the case lend support to the opinion that we are not dealing here with a kind of impersonal physical force which perhaps sometime in the future will fall within the scope of physics although its operation is not now understood. If the Seaford disturbances were not fraudulent—and no evidence of fraud was found—they clearly make a proper claim upon the interest of parapsychologists.

It must be kept in mind that all such investigations as conducted to date rank as exploratory rather than as conclusive. There was, for example, no disturbance in the Seaford case which the investigators could observe under conditions as good as those that can be produced in the laboratory. However free from any suggestion of fraud or known physical explanation this case as a whole may have been, the investigation was largely based on testimony rather than on firsthand observations under controlled experimental conditions. Thus our report concerning what took place in the Seaford case was inconclusive. It would be an improper application of scientific method to attempt to go further on the basis of such material.

But science consists of more than reaching conclusions. One of its important functions is the appraisal of problems that might justify further study. The investigation of data bearing upon a problem that needs clarification is an indispensable link in the chain of scientific progress. The observations which suggest that spontaneous outbursts of "mind over matter" may be happening in at least some of these so-called poltergeist cases present such a problem and the Seaford case may have come closer than any other to supplying the necessary link between the uncontrolled, question-raising events of the natural life situation and the controlled, question-answering events of the laboratory experiments on PK.

But the Seaford case may in the long run be remembered as an episode that contributed to the advance of the psi revolution by serving as a gauge of public interest in such matters. We reached—I repeat—no conclusion regarding the case itself, but one conclusion was brought home to us with the force of a new volcano erupting in one's own back yard: people everywhere are intensely interested in such unexplained human experiences as the Herrmanns had to endure! And they are interested in the scientific approach to these things—to the whole problem of psi phenomena—as shown by the fact that it was not until the two halves of the "atomic charge," the case itself on the one hand and the investigator from the Parapsychology Laboratory on the other hand, came together that the potential energy exceeded the critical level and there resulted the explosion of publicity heard around the world.

Because of the attention this case received, it has already helped to bring several later ones to the attention of interested research workers while the disturbances were still taking place. Unfortunately, it is not possible to report that any of these subsequent studies has been any more conclusive than was our investigation of the Seaford case. But scientists working on the frontiers of knowledge dare not set deadlines for themselves in their struggles to discover Nature's closely guarded secrets. The researcher must always press on toward his goal, learning from his own failures and retreating only far enough to escape from the box canyon into which his latest wrong turn led him.

6

Precognition:
The Facts and the Furor

President Lincoln, shortly before his assassination, had a vivid dream in which he apparently foresaw his own death. The circumstances under which he told this dream and the manner in which the record was preserved endow the incident with more than ordinary interest.

The occasion when Lincoln reluctantly told about his unusual experience was a gathering in the White House. He and Mrs. Lincoln were celebrating with a few close friends the news of Lee's surrender. The President seemed unusually silent and morose, and remarks from Mrs. Lincoln led up to his relating the dream. These are Lincoln's words as recorded by Ward Hill Lamon, U.S. marshal for the District of Columbia, who was present and who wrote out his account of the incident the same night.

"About ten days ago, I retired very late. I had been waiting for important dispatches. . . . I soon began to dream. There seemed to be a deathlike stillness about me. Then I heard subdued sobs, as if a number of people were weeping. I thought I left my bed and wandered downstairs.

"There the silence was broken by the same pitiful sobbing, but the mourners were invisible. I went from room to room. No living person was in sight, but the same mournful sounds of distress met me as I passed along.

"It was light in all the rooms; every object was familiar to me, but where were all the people who were grieving as if their hearts would break?

"I was puzzled and alarmed. What could be the meaning of all this? Determined to find the cause of a state of affairs so mysterious, and so shocking, I kept on until I arrived in the East Room, which I entered. There I met with a sickening surprise. Before me was a catafalque, on which rested a corpse in funeral vestments. Around it were stationed soldiers who were acting as guards; and there was a throng of people, some gazing mournfully upon the corpse, whose face was covered, others weeping pitifully.

"'Who is dead in the White House?' I demanded of one of the soldiers.

"'The President,' was his answer. 'He was killed by an assassin.'"

It is too much to expect that famous men should all provide precognitive dreams involving world-shaking events. But the number of cases from people in all walks of life is large enough to raise and to underscore the question of whether precognition occurs. Some general estimate of how widespread such experiences are can be formed on the basis of facts already available.

We may start with the indications that many people have had unusual experiences that were convincing to themselves as examples of psi occurrences. The S.P.R. investigators, we may recall, found in their census of hallucinations that about ten per cent of those questioned admitted to having had at least one such experience. Dr. W. F. Prince in the U.S.A. later conducted a similar survey of people whose names were taken from Who's Who and he found the same general level of affirmative answers.

We may go on, next, to the fact reported by Dr. Louisa Rhine. She found that approximately two fifths of the cases in her large collection involved precognition. Unlike the experiences involving ordinary ESP, most of the reports of precognition were dream cases. A personal experience that predicted the future is something that most people are reluctant to talk about. For this reason the surveys are likely to lead us to underestimate the number of persons who have had such experiences in their daily lives. I venture, however, to make a rough guess that the individuals who have convincingly precognized one or more future events are at least as common as left-handed people!

That spontaneous cases raise the question of whether precognition occurs is clear. But how does the investigator get beyond the original question? He must find a *method* before he can make any real progress toward a scientific solution of the problem.

The most obvious approach, of course, is to try to investigate the cases themselves, in the same general manner as the early workers in the S.P.R. studied cases as evidence for telepathy. Indeed, over the years many cases were collected by the societies on both sides of the Atlantic, and their files contained the usual percentage of precognitive experiences. In the twenties, H. F. Saltmarsh assembled and tried to assess the best S.P.R. cases in this category. The outcome of his study was very impressive. If it had been concerned with any ordinary scientific problem, there seems little doubt that it would have won wide and favorable attention among scientists. But—precognition! *Precognition!?* Are not people having millions of dreams every night? And out of this vast number are they not likely to read meaning into a few when something later happens that appears to coincide with their dreams to some degree, as it is bound by chance to do?

One thing, at least, seemed clear to the experiment-minded research worker: it would take more than dreams to prove precognition. But how might this problem be approached? It occurred to Dr. Rhine, once the distinction was drawn between telepathy and clairvoyance, that testing for the principle back of precognitive experiences in everyday life might work, just as tests for ESP had proved successful during the early years of the S.P.R. He took encouragement from the fact that the ESP tests over the years had apparently not been affected by distance. If ESP were free from limitations of space, should it not also work across the barrier of time?

As a start toward answering this question, why not turn the ordinary ESP test around and have the subjects call the cards *before* they were shuffled? This was tried at first on the simplest level possible: the subjects were asked to make their calls for the order of cards in a shuffled pack *not as it was but as the order would be after the cards were cut*. Then the subjects themselves cut the pack a few times before the hits were checked. At the start, the subjects worked alone and did all their own checking, which was all right for the initial, exploratory stage. Later the experimenter did the shuffling of the cards and cut them after the subject's calls had been made and before he had a chance to see them.

The first precognition tests were made with the subjects who had previously done well in the Duke ESP research. But the sad fact was that the subjects were all declining in their level of scoring by the time the witnessed precognition tests were introduced. The first blush of excitement had naturally faded with time. Not too surprisingly, the precognition results were no better than the subjects could achieve in other ESP tests carried out at the same general time. But the results were nevertheless encouraging as explorations, all of the witnessed results together gaining the level of significance represented by the chance odds of 1 in more than 35,000 such batches of trials.

But then came one of those moments when hindsight is better than foresight, which research workers learn to live through as a normal hazard of their trade. (In this instance the setback, as is fortunately often true in science, proved to be the spur to greater effort and achievement.) One of the graduate students in the laboratory, Mr. B. M. Smith, suggested that he would like to have a shuffled pack of ESP cards take the place of the subject's calls, and he would attempt to shuffle another pack so as to get a good score when the two orders of cards were compared. Obviously, if he were successful over a series of runs to a degree that chance could not adequately explain, the significant results that the subjects' calls in the earlier tests had given when matched against cards someone had shuffled afterward could not be used as evidence of precognition.

Mr. Smith proved his point. The investigators of precognition therefore had to find some way of making the order of future targets immune from the "ESP shuffle" effect. This led to only the first one of a variety of advances in precognition testing procedures, each step aimed at making it more certain that the cards were not being influenced volitionally after the calls were recorded so as to produce a non-chance number of hits.

To get around the ESP shuffle, the experimenters introduced mechanical shuffling machines to rearrange the cards. To make matters even more secure, the pack as it was taken from the shuffling machine was cut according to the sum of the faces on a number of dice that were thrown from a cup or tumbled in another machine. Again, the precognition results were beyond the reasonable range of chance fluctuation—not high in terms of the average rate of hitting, but sustained over a long series of trials so that the final chance odds were clearly beyond the accepted standards of statistical significance.

Then came the experimental evidence for PK. "So what?" you may ask. So the precognition results were again in doubt! If PK could influence the fall of dice in an experiment designed to test the psychokinesis hypothesis, what was to keep it from influencing the fall of the cards in the shuffling machine and the fall of dice for the final cut of the pack? Of course, this would be to assume that the person using PK in this way was also using clairvoyance to read the cards (and the calls as well if he needed to do so). He needed this information in order to know what PK result on the dice would give the kind of "precognition" score desired. Perhaps this all seems a bit farfetched, but what could be more farfetched than the notion that precognition is possible?

Parapsychologists must show, as their first qualification, virtually unlimited patience. So the research workers gave a further tug to their thinking caps and decided that some larger and more complicated series of future events than the fall of dice—something occurring on a national or terrestrial scale—should be used to give the final cut to the target pack. For a time the target-selection procedure used was the newspaper cut. The target pack was shuffled either before or immediately after the subject had made his calls, but the final order to be used was determined by a random cut made on the basis of a particular set of figures *that would be printed in the newspaper of the following day.* Suitable figures that appeared regularly in the paper were selected for use in the experiment, such as the daily report of local temperature or the market report of the number of dozens of hen eggs sold on the produce market. These figures involved information concerning events that always came later than the time when the subject made his calls.

Again, the precognition results in some of the experiments were consistently and significantly unlike scores that would be expected from chance. But there were many times when the results were indistinguishable from what chance would be expected to produce, and these served to warn the experimenters against taking the outcome of the psi tests for granted. Nevertheless, when we took the bad with the good, the over-all effect was one that students of the research could not easily dismiss.

But the precognition hypothesis places a great strain upon the modern educated mind. This means that the evidence in return must be able to stand a more than ordinarily severe stress test. So the research in precognition has continued, most investigators frankly admitting that more evidence is needed. As this has been sought, two main further innovations in the target-finding procedures have been introduced. Both of these were suggested because a method was needed for providing quicker checking of the results than the newspaper cut provided, and not because the latter was inadequate on theoretical grounds.

The first change was one proposed by Dr. Rhine. He suggested that a complicated calculation, worked out on an electric calculator, should be interposed between the throwing of the dice and the final cut. The numbers from the faces of the dice would represent only the starting point for the calculation, and certain prescribed digits in the final answer given by the electric calculator would be used to cut the pack (or to get a random entry point into a statistical table of random numbers to find the digits that would be translated by a set code into the precognition ESP-symbol targets). The procedure was described in detail in advance and carried out strictly by the rules laid down before starting the experiment to avoid the possibility that any sort of influence other than precognition could consistently produce extra-chance scores. The calculation done by the machine was so difficult that it effectively blocked out the information required for applying PK to get favorable numbers on the dice *unless the person using it also showed precognition for the outcome of the complicated computation.* The alternative mentioned in the italicized part of the last sentence need not concern us greatly at this stage of the research, for to fall back upon that interpretation would be to concede the precognition hypothesis which the experiment was designed to prove!

The other method introduced to permit quicker checking of the results was one that I myself first suggested away back in the summer of 1936. This was shortly after we began to fret about uncontrolled, contaminating PK in the determination of precognition targets. I proposed that we use a sufficiently large number of dice at one toss, such as six, and add together their faces to get the final cutting place in the shuffled pack. This number of dice, *all of which would have to be controlled to control the sum,* would place such a heavy burden upon PK as to render that hypothesis only a remote possibility. The reason why this is true is that we have never found any evidence that PK subjects can influence dice perfectly. Just one die falling at random would nullify the influence of PK, even if it had worked perfectly on all five of the other dice in the toss!

In those days we were being extra severe with ourselves as self-critics. For that reason we put this idea on the shelf as being not so good as we needed in the uphill fight we were facing to get a hearing for the results of the precognition experiments.

When I offered the same idea again more than twenty years later it met with more favor. The reasons why were two: first, we had almost entirely gone over to the use of random number tables as the basis of getting the order of future targets for the subject's precognition calls, and this placed a much greater strain upon the amount of clairvoyance required if PK were to be used; second, the table of 1,000,000 random digits which we were accustomed to using required that a more complex set of six dice be used to get an entry point for the targets, and this similarly put a heavier strain upon the PK component of the ESP-PK counterexplanation to precognition. Clearly, results by either the computer method or the dice-shaken-in-a-closed-box method were important as further evidence of precognition in the laboratory.

And what were the results by these two new methods?

When the computer idea was introduced at Duke in the early fifties, it made precognition tests seem attractive to a number of the members of the laboratory staff. In fact, it became a sort of rage to do the tests with the new method, and investigators plunged in without much forethought—certainly in most cases they were not demonstrating precognition regarding the outcome of their own experiments! The upshot was that they did not feel the same urgency about publishing their findings as they had felt in seeking them.

After three of four years an experimenter who used a more suitable subject in his experiment obtained results that were worth publishing. I urged upon him the necessity of taking account of the background of unpublished work in the introduction to his report of his own findings. A total of fifty-eight precognition series had been carried out with the calculation procedure. These ranged in size from ten to more than one hundred runs. When they were evaluated in terms of the amount of fluctuation from chance which they showed from series to series over the data as a whole, the chance odds were found to be 1 in 50. Thus even this motley collection of exploratory tests was sufficiently impressive to add a bit to the evidence that something more than chance was involved in the efforts of the subjects to predict the future orders of ESP cards.

Since that time (1955), the efforts to do further precognition tests have been planned with more care, the approach has been less scattered in character, and the reporting has kept up with the attempts. The trend, on the whole, has been toward a steady mounting of evidence for precognition which bids fair to satisfy in time the most skeptical (provided he is open-minded) student of the findings.

To some extent the greater success of precognition tests in recent years may be due to the use of more suitable subjects: people who had a strong interest, sometimes coupled with a high degree of confidence in their own precognitive abilities. Dr. G. L. Mangan worked with one such selected subject, a woman in San Diego, who called five runs of ESP cards a day, five days a week, for four weeks, aiming at targets that would be selected in the Duke Parapsychology Laboratory when she had finished. The targets were taken from a random number book after an entering place had been selected by the method using the electric calculator. Following the lead of Dr. Soal in England, Dr. Mangan checked each call (except the first and last ones in the run, as you will readily understand) for success in hitting three targets: the one directly alongside it in the target list; the one just before it; and the one just after it. The outstanding success came in the third category, which is called forward displacement, and for this the chance odds were 1 in 1667.

Mrs. Winnifred Nielsen, another Duke laboratory staff member, picked out a personal friend in a distant state as a subject, someone who was especially interested in precognition. A conservative statement of the chance odds in her experiment is 1 in 90.

Dr. Karlis Osis, also working at the time as a member of the Duke group, tested a special subject who made her calls at her home in New York. The total series of nearly 240 runs gave results that were *so consistently below chance* that they would occur by mere coincidence on the average only 1 time in 1380 such series.

Miss Margaret Anderson carried out an experiment with a special subject, Miss Rose Hynes, a Duke student who was going to study for a year in Paris. While she was there she called cards to be checked later at Duke. Her results in ninety runs, which were checked by two experimenters, gave chance odds of 1 in 64. Half of these runs were checked a year later than the others, and these gave *better* scores, with odds of 1 in 450.

But not all the successful experiments have depended upon the use of selected subjects. One has been carried out with a group of subjects in the classroom, and two others have involved special efforts to achieve favorable psychological conditions with unselected volunteers. The group experiment was carried out with a sixth-grade class, two testing sessions a month over the school year. Again, Miss Anderson was the initiator of the experiment, and she linked up with Mrs. Elsie Gregory, a classroom teacher in Wheaton, Illinois. The fluctuation from session to session was so great—sometimes too high for chance to explain; sometimes too low—that the chance odds for the total experiment were 1 in more than 10,000.

The other two significant precognition experiments which used a number of subjects were done with Duke University students. In one study, by Mr. Michael Sanders, favorable conditions were carefully established in exploratory tests, and then in a crucial test series the experimenter predicted that he would get significant results and he made good to the tune of 1 in 1250 chance odds. In the second experiment, Dr. John Freeman challenged his subjects to show that they could do well on precognition tests because this was the most common single type of spontaneous psi experience in everyday life. The subjects obliged in the precognition series with chance odds of 1 in 1000, while in a clairvoyance series they were near the chance level.

As I write, I know of only one precognition test conducted during this period which produced only chance results. (This is not to claim, however, that I know of everything that has been attempted.) And there have been, to my knowledge, other experiments that *were* successful that have not yet reached the point of being published.

The foregoing bits of laboratory, experimental evidence, added to and reinforced by the evidence from everyday life, comprise my own reason for saying that the idea that the mind can somehow penetrate the future cannot be shoved aside or ignored. Granting that the evidence is strong, what are we to make of it?

The answer to this question comes in two parts.

The first is concerned with the complications which precognition has made for the psi researchers. This will take a bit of time in the telling.

Then there is the question of what precognition means philosophically and in terms of ethics—the question of freedom of choice in a world with a predictable future. Does precognition offer us with one hand undeniable evidence of the existence of mind and with the other hand take away the last semblance of freedom of action in the face of a fatalistically determined existence? This point, in turn, will deserve some words of comment.

Establishing the ESP of future events caused real difficulties for the investigators. This is already apparent from the number of steps through which the experimental procedure was advanced before a reasonably satisfactory method of testing for precogniton was found. In fact, it appeared that this process—the prediction of the future—almost had the property of a universal psi solvent, so difficult was it to find a procedure which would adequately contain the effect that we wished to isolate for study. Just as the precognition hypothesis tended to dissolve our *experimental safeguards* against alternative interpretations, so also did the finding of clear evidence for ESP of future events tend to dissolve the special features of earlier psi experiments by which the investigators had distinguished, as they thought, among telepathy, clairvoyance, and PK.

If precognition occurs, how may we be sure that the subject in a pure telepathy test was really reading the mind of the sender? Even though there were no physical cards, what was to say that the subject did not, by precognitive clairvoyance, delve into the future and read the record of the target which was written down *after* the subject's call?

And, similarly, what was to say that clairvoyance was not really precognitive telepathy, achieved by dipping into the future to read what would be in the experimenter's mind at the time the calls and cards were checked?

And what was to say that PK was PK at all? Might it not, in view of the great leveler, precognition, be simply a use of the mind's ability to look into the future to choose the right target face of the die or the right moment for throwing to achieve an over-chance score?

Scores of pages have been used in the parapsychological literature to discuss these thorny issues. In view of this fact, I hope I may be allowed four, even in a popular book.

Clearing telepathy of the charge of being merely precognitive clairvoyance required only the necessary amount of ingenuity and an ample amount of the unlimited patience credited to the parapsychologists. To achieve this purpose when one sender worked alone was relatively easy: he needed only to concentrate sufficiently so that he did not have to write down the targets or to make at any time any objective sign of what they were.

But this was not sufficient for conclusive proof, which required that two people should be able to check the results to insure accuracy. This was accomplished by having them establish a code of numbers to represent the five ESP symbols. They made no record of what the code was, but agreed upon it by referring in terms that were meaningful only to themselves to memories of experiences which they had shared.

For example, experimenter A might say: "Let's have the digit representing the number of cars involved in a wreck we saw recently stand for star," to which experimenter B either assented or gave a countersuggestion if he did not remember the wreck. This process was repeated until each digit, 1 to 5, meant a different one of the five symbols in a code known only to the two experimenters.

Once the code was established in this manner, the sender could use a random order of the five digits as a basis for thinking of the ESP symbols in accordance with the associations mentally agreed upon. Then, at the end of each run, the sender counted up the total score, doing so without indicating where each hit occurred. After that the calls were handed over to the second experimenter, who also counted up the total score. To keep from giving the code away, he also avoided marking the individual hits.

Two significant "pure telepathy" experiments were carried through by this general method. The first was done at Duke by Miss Elizabeth McMahan and Dr. Betty Humphrey. The other was done in England by Dr. S. G. Soal and Mr. F. Bateman. Both studies gave significant results but the latter had the advantage of a single outstanding ESP subject, Mrs. Gloria Stewart, and it achieved, not surprisingly, a much higher level of significance, the chance odds being 1 in 100,000,000,000.

Theoretically, freeing clairvoyance of being a mere pretender—precognitive telepathy in disguise—is a much simpler task. The ideal method, unfortunately, has not yet been done—at least, those who have attempted it have not had the right subjects or the right conditions for getting ESP results at the time. The ideal test for "pure clairvoyance" would be to use a method which automatically conceals the identity of the targets for the individual trials but leaves a record of the total number of hits at the end of the run. In this way there would never be any record of the physical events at some future time which could serve as the targets for precognitive telepathy, such as at the time of the checking of the scores. For example, a subject might attempt to sort unseen marbles of five different colors into five covered containers, one for each color. At the end of the run the number right could be counted, but there would be no way of telling which trials had been right and which wrong. Thus there would not be any future *order* of the marbles for precognitive telepathy to predict, since the order would not be preserved for the checking of the results. But, as I have said, the first significant test of pure clairvoyance with an ideal kind of apparatus or procedure remains to be done.

But clairvoyance has not fared too badly in precognition, even so. Some of the test procedures are such that the true order of the target cards is not preserved for the checkup. These are experiments in which the subject sorts the cards into five piles, attempting to put all of the symbols of one kind into its own special pile as marked by a key card bearing that symbol. The only reason why this is not an ideal test of pure clairvoyance is that cards are not like marbles: they do not automatically lose track of the order in which they were placed down. A fairly strong case has been made for pure clairvoyance, in spite of the furor stirred up by precognition, on the basis of the present evidence. But the challenge of a clear-cut test of clairvoyance in which the results stand clear of any need for argument is one that beckons to the research worker who wants to blaze a new trail.

The case for PK against precognition is strongest, in my judgment, from the evidence given by the highly regular, rhythmic up-and-down effects that occur within the column, or series of columns (set), of the records. These regular changes are not characteristic of the kinds of results one would find in PK results if they represented merely the selection of the lucky target face for a series of "chance" throws. The PK data represent not merely an over-all good score, as the precognition counterexplanation supposes, but they show that something was happening to the dice in a graded fashion on a trial-to-trial basis. In view of the conditions imposed in many of the experiments, this *something* could only be PK.

But the furor over PK and precognition spreads in both directions. In recent months there has been a furious discussion of whether precognition itself has really been established, in spite of all the efforts made in the experimental procedures to exclude the alternative possibilities of PK and ESP. This furor was initiated in the *Journal of the Society for Psychical Research* by Mr. W. G. Roll, who has suggested that what seems like a precognition of the future in the case material drawn from everyday life may be considered instead as evidence of an already existing pattern of events which is working itself out in nature. This pattern, he suggests, spreads an influence which may affect someone's experience before it affects in a corresponding way the pattern of events in the outside world. When this happens, Mr. Roll says, it gives rise to the conviction that the future has been foreseen. Regarding the experimental results, the question is raised whether they may not, after all, be due to other factors like PK and ESP in spite of our best efforts to exclude them.

Others have jumped into this discussion to make it an intellectual, free-for-all debate. I mention the matter here not because I agree with Mr. Roll, for I do not. Rather, it is interesting as an example of the thinking that parapsychologists must occasionally do in relation to the problems on their most advanced frontiers. It shows the degree to which they are still searching for ways of coming to grips with the difficult issues upon which the research is attempting to focus. We need not despair for the psi revolution in view of this state of affairs. It only shows that the various contenders are taking their jobs seriously and that they realize not only the importance of the problems with which they are concerned but also (and especially) the importance of not allowing any suggested solutions to go unchallenged. Scientists seek not finality of discovery, but only the privilege of working unceasingly for better ways of viewing that ideal goal, truth, which may be approached but never overtaken.

In this spirit, I venture to raise a few queries about the bearing of precognition (assuming that it occurs) on the question of freedom of choice. If something has been precognized, does this mean that it must inevitably come to pass? If so, does this mean that we have no freedom of choice in regard to the future—at least, no choice as regards that part of the future that has been precognized? In much that has been said on this knotty problem, there has been a general implication that precognition implies a fixed future and that this would deny freedom of choice. May this not be an unwarranted implication?

Will you grant that precognition, by definition, is *a direct perception of a future event which is beyond the reach of inference or which is not brought about to fulfill the prediction?* If you will, then precognition is a *response* to a specific future *something.* This means that a relation is necessarily involved: the cognizing subject on the one hand, and the cognized future event on the other.

For the precognition to be real, both members of this relationship must be a part of reality. (If the event apparently precognized does not actually take place at some time in the future, then we *must* concede that there was no genuine act of precognition.)

But does the fact that an event has been precognized tell us anything about *how* it will eventually be determined? What difference does it make to the precognition process whether the event comes about as the result of a free choice or is purely physicalistically determined? Why should anyone suppose that future events of the former kind are any less available as precognition targets than are events that occur solely through physical action? In other words, can precognition itself tell us anything about whether the foreseen event belongs to the one or the other of these two categories? May it not be telling us only that there is *a* future—a future which we all *feel* that we are helping to create by the choices we are freely making?

Suppose, for example, that I precognize seeing a man falling past my hotel window. Can we reasonably think that this act of precognition depends in any way upon the nature of the events that will lead up to the fulfillment of my ESP of the future? Why should it make any difference to the precognizability of the situation how the man would happen to fall? Would he be any harder to precognize at the moment of going past my window if he had been pushed than if he had been struck from a scaffold by a bolt of lightning? It is the *fall* that I precognize, and from this experience alone I cannot distinguish between volitional or purely accidental causes of the accident. Whether or not the act was one of free choice is simply not relevant to the fact that I somehow knew in advance that I would witness the fall itself taking place.

Now suppose that my experience was a *genuine* instance of precognition on my part. Could I make the fall *not* occur by doing anything to prevent it? But here is a contradiction. My experience could not be *genuine* unless I later actually did see a man fall past my window. So if I work "successfully" to prevent a fall from taking place, I am acting on a false belief that I had actually foreseen such an accident.

It appears, therefore, that in those instances when people feel they have avoided some serious crisis which they believed they had precognized, they must have been mistaken regarding their prediction. A genuine act of precognition, once it has occurred, is a part of the past, and we cannot nullify it by anything that we can do in the future. To say we can do this is tantamount to claiming that we can change the past. What this adds up to is simply the view that precognition and freedom of choice are separate questions. When they have been linked together, it has been an unnecessary tangling of two issues, each of which is thorny enough by itself!

But in another very real sense, the occurrence of precognition does bear upon the question of freedom of the will. In precognition we have the clearest evidence parapsychology has to offer that mind is not a mere illusion, that it is *there*, a reality which is beyond the explanatory principles of purely physical science. Precognition thus gives the strongest support to the idea of freedom from a closed circle of physical causation. It shows that man, endowed with his psi capacities, has his mind which, *to some degree*, sets him free from complete physical bondage.

7

Does Mind Survive Death?

In 1885, William James, professor of psychology at Harvard University, heard from his wife's mother and sister that they had gone out of curiosity, one after the other, to visit a spiritualist medium in Boston. They said that the medium, Mrs. Leonore Piper, had given them names and detailed personal facts regarding deceased members of their family. This information convinced them that she had some unexplained, remarkable way of knowing such things.

Even though James argued with his in-laws that their experience with Mrs. Piper probably had a normal explanation, this did not stop him from going with his wife a short time later to visit the medium. Their experience likewise was very impressive. In spite of the pains taken not to let Mrs. Piper know who was coming for the "sitting" and the care exercised not to give any clues after they arrived, Mrs. Piper, in her trance state, gave them names and descriptions of several deceased relatives. The information was so exact as to leave no doubt in the minds of the two visitors that the medium, when she went into a trance state and then wrote automatically to answer questions or even to volunteer information, was accurately identifying members of their families. As was usually the case with the spiritualistic mediums of the day, the information was worded as if it was coming from a "spirit control" who appeared to take over Mrs. Piper's faculties during her trance. The so-called control claimed to be relaying information from deceased loved ones and occasionally seemed to be able to help the relative or friend on the other side to communicate directly.

Later James summed up his opinion of Mrs. Piper's abilities as follows:

My impression after this first visit was that Mrs. P. was either possessed of supernormal powers, or knew the members of my wife's family by sight and had by some lucky coincidence become acquainted with such a multitude of their domestic circumstances as to produce the startling impression which she did. My later knowledge of her sittings and personal acquaintance with her has led me absolutely to reject the latter explanation, and to believe that she has supernormal powers.

Being of a truly scientific mind and recognizing the importance of the view of the matter which he had reluctantly come to hold, James did not let the case of Mrs. Piper rest there. Instead, he brought her to the attention of the members of the recently formed Society for Psychical Research in England and took an active part in arranging to have her visit them for the purpose of making further, more formal investigations of her mediumistic trance results. Thus began in full earnest, four years after the founding of the S.P.R., the scientific study of the phenomena of spiritualism.

The spiritualistic movement, indeed, had from the start of the S.P.R. appeared to the members of the society to deserve scientific attention. The religious cult had become widespread during the third quarter of the nineteenth century, and the founders of the S.P.R., in the spirit of keeping their minds open to all possible psi effects, had set up a committee for the investigation of spiritualistic phenomena. The popular interest in these matters undoubtedly helped to set the stage for the scientific efforts that were to loom so large over the next few decades. The study of mediumship came, in fact, to dominate the work of the Society for Psychical Research. There is a time and tide in research as well as in the other affairs of men. This was well illustrated by the fact that, following the discovery of Mrs. Piper, other professional mediums were soon found who were willing to lend themselves for the purposes of serious study.

As a result there was no lack of opportunity to push these investigations as far as the research workers might wish and were able to carry them. There even emerged, before the end of the century, a group of "self-made" or "self-discovered" sensitives (the scientific term for mediums) within the membership of the S.P.R. itself. More and more, the investigators came to feel that they had found a rich vein of ore from which the psi yield seemed to be very high and which, unlike the experimental tests they had already tried, had unlimited reserves. There seemed to be no reason to fear that the best sensitives would lose their powers as the subjects in telepathy experiments were found to do.

But the attraction to the investigation of mediumship was not merely a practical one. The information coming out of the sittings held promise of leading to discoveries of the greatest importance from the point of view of the major objective of the S.P.R.: that of pursuing by the methods of objective research the investigation of those factors in man that most sharply challenge interpretation in terms of physical law. If, as appeared on the surface, the mediums were really serving as channels through which deceased loved ones were communicating with those they had left behind, then there must be something about man's personality that is capable of surviving death. This something could not be physical in terms of physics as we know it today and as we are able to conceive of its becoming. Proof of survival would therefore constitute final proof of the existence of psi and mind. This was the important *scientific* bearing that the investigators of the survival question thought of their work as having.

Furthermore, if the evidence of life after death should be established beyond any point of doubt, this scientific discovery was seen as a tremendous advance in philosophical and religious thought. Survival, which had so long been a belief to be taken on religious faith, would become a universal truth and ethic.

(There are scientists today, some even in parapsychology, who consider that it is improper to raise this question as one for serious research consideration. For example, an esteemed scientific colleague with whom I discussed our field in my visit to the new laboratory for the investigation of ESP at the University of Leningrad has recently expressed such an opinion. In an English-language review of one of his books dealing with parapsychology he is quoted as suggesting that research interest in the question of survival will delay the acceptance of psi as a legitimate branch of research. I respect his right to his opinion, as I hope he respects my right to mine, which is that science, and particularly parapsychology, cannot afford to exclude any meaningful question about the universe as being out of bounds for research. There is always the risk that questions may be raised before it is possible to deal with them effectively. Or it is possible that the research worker raising a particular question may be mistaken in thinking that it is a meaningful one. But in either case the most that should be charged against the venturesome researcher is that he might have found a better use of his time. This can scarcely be said regarding anyone who undertakes research on the survival problem. If a positive answer to the question were found, it would obviously be of overpowering importance. And even if in the end the answer were a negative one that runs counter to most religious beliefs, the achievement of sound scientific knowledge to this effect is better than ignorance.)

The amount of serious thought and work already invested by scientists on the survival question is enough to compel us to consider what has been done on this problem. And until we reach the stage of having a scientific solution one way or the other, the survival question is most definitely one that must be pursued. While the present facts do not add up to a final answer, they advance us toward one. What are the methods that have been followed thus far, what are the results, and what prospects can we now see for our ever knowing whether mind survives death?

The serious discussions that have been published on this general topic add up to thousands of pages, but I'm going to try to cover it in a short chapter. Since the largest amount of effort has gone into the study of mediumship, it is appropriate to consider first the kinds of evidence which such studies have yielded and the tentative conclusions to which the investigators were led. After that I will discuss other kinds of experience that raise the question and strongly suggest, if taken at face value, that personality does continue beyond death. Then we must give some thought to how the status of this problem has changed over the past thirty years. Does the progress that has been made during this period in the laboratory studies of the psi capacities of the living bring the answer to the survival question any closer or make it more remote?

From the beginning the investigators recognized that the first question was whether the trance material received through a medium contained *real* information, and not just lucky guesses. Deciding this issue appeared to most of the workers to be the easiest part of their task, since it seemed to them that many of the names and detailed descriptions of personal circumstances were too unmistakably accurate to attribute the results to chance coincidence. We have already seen how William James quickly was won over to this point of view. Most of the leading members of the S.P.R. followed him in this judgment as they worked with Mrs. Piper and other mediums who became available over the next few decades.

But granting that the mediums were providing accurate information to which they did not have access through normal sensory means, from what source were they getting it? Was it coming from the surviving minds of the deceased loved ones as the spiritualistic interpretation would hold and as the records from the sittings themselves represented to be the case? Or was the source some living mind from which the information was received by the medium through telepathy and simply dramatized to make it seem to be coming "from the other side?" The investigators recognized that it would be necessary to exclude the possibility of telepathy from the living before they could reach any positive conclusion regarding survival. But they did not feel that it was necessary to worry about the possibilities that mediums might get their information through clairvoyance or precognition, because they did not take these forms of ESP very seriously.

A major controversy over whether telepathy from the living or survival was the interpretation of the results soon sprang up among those who agreed that the mediums had some unusual way of revealing facts that they could not have known through their senses. Some investigators were, not surprisingly, inclined to accept the ability of mediums to give obscure but detailed personal data as proof of contact with surviving personalities. Others said that as long as it seemed even remotely possible to credit the success to telepathy from the living, scientific logic required the acceptance of this explanation couched in terms of a known principle.

Then a new development took place in the investigation of mediumship, an advance which had the appearance of being planned for the purpose of making it more difficult to attribute the results to telepathy from the living. Among those who were most deeply immersed in the first years of survival research in the S.P.R. were some outstanding classical scholars, such as F. W. H. Myers and A. W. Verrall. This fact is important in relation to a change in the kind of evidence found in some of the sittings after Myers' death in 1901. Not only did what purported to be communications from Myers start coming through different mediums, but these soon took the form of references to obscure items of information drawn from the classics. This information was beyond the education and normal knowledge of mediums like Mrs. Piper. In most instances it was beyond the understanding of the sitters and note takers as well. Only after the records were studied by living classical scholars were the "messages" recognized.

These sittings were discovered to have produced what seemed to be deliberately contrived classical puzzles which were interpreted as especially strong evidence of survival. It is easy to understand the reason why it was difficult for the investigators to take seriously the alternative interpretation of telepathy from the living, for from what *living* person's mind could the information be coming? (Not from the mind of any *disinterested* living scholar, because telepathy, they thought, involved a need on the part of the sender to communicate as well as a suitable person to receive the message.) What was more natural than that Myers and Sidgwick, both of whom had died recently, and other classical scholars who were members of the S.P.R. and who died a few years later, should continue to be interested in proving that the personality survives death—if they had discovered at first hand that it is indeed true? And what better way of serving this worthy cause than to design experiments from the other side which would point forcefully to their own surviving minds as the most likely source of the information coming through the medium?

The evidence conveyed in these classical literary puzzles reached an advanced stage. Those who were slaving over the analysis and interpretation of the records discovered what they named the "cross-correspondences." A part of the literary puzzle was found in the record of one medium, such as that of a sitting held in America with Mrs. Piper, and other parts of the puzzle came through one or more other mediums who were in England or India. The mediums were not in touch with one another in any ordinary sense. The evidence, said the scholars who had the responsibility of studying the records, indicated that some mind or minds that were steeped in the classics had deliberately devised this scheme to prove that the results could not be due to telepathy on the part of one medium. The plan and the initiative for the experiment, it seemed, had to be found elsewhere, and who could have managed it if not the deceased scholars who were claiming the credit and offering the feat as proof of their continued existence after death?

This material is extremely complicated, and great ingenuity was required in making the analyses and interpreting the findings. Few people could claim, even at the time, that they were equal to making an adequate appraisal of the results. But the people who found the evidence in the records and reported it were, themselves, first-rate scholars whose integrity was beyond question. They gained a lot of support for their interpretations among people who were capable of assimilating the findings and who took the trouble to do so. Yet it seems that Dr. Thouless was generally correct when he said, many years after this type of evidence had ceased to accumulate, that the cross-correspondences suffered from the experimental defect of being *too* complicated! Science requires experiments that are simple and straightforward and easily interpretable, especially in research that is aimed at advancing knowledge beyond what is perhaps its most impenetrable frontier.

The developments we have traced thus far in the methods of studying mediumship were largely unplanned and opportunistic. That is, the investigators simply took advantage of the phenomena that were presented to them and only imposed upon them their skill as observers and their judgment in the interpretation of the results. Even the beginnings of what could properly be called an experiment as represented by the cross-correspondences were not planned by the S.P.R. research workers—at least, not consciously so. (Later there was a suggestion that Mrs. A. W. Verrall, one of the mediums who had some knowledge of the classics, might unconsciously have been the instigator of the scheme.) Two further developments which simply showed up in the mediumistic records also had the appearance of having been initiated "from the other side." These were book tests and newspaper tests.

The book tests were for the purpose of providing simple and direct evidence of a sort that could not be attributed to telepathy from the living. The person who claimed to be communicating through the medium would attempt to prove that the information was coming from himself rather than by telepathy from some living person's mind by referring the sitter to a page in a particular book. The sitter was told that on the designated page he would find information that would give convincing evidence that the communicator speaking through the medium was real and not merely a fantasy of the trance state bolstered by telepathic powers. For example, the personality that appeared to be communicating might prompt the medium's "control" (the trance personality acting as his go-between and interpreter during the sitting) to say: "He says if you will look in the fifth book from the left on the top shelf of his bookcase, on page 172 you will find a description that applies to his condition toward the end of his life." The reference, when it is later looked up, might be found to contain a description of the final stages of the unusual illness from which the communicator had died. Chronologically, this type of evidence followed upon the cross-correspondences. It began in the teens and appeared prominently in mediumistic records from then until the early thirties. It did not, of course, eliminate the possibility of clairvoyance, but at that time this did not seem like a serious shortcoming.

In a similar way the newspaper tests were introduced during the same period. The medium would refer the sitter to a particular page and column of the next day's newspaper for some significant information. The objective here was to introduce still stronger safeguards against an explanation in terms of the ordinary ESP powers that the medium might possess. The newspaper "message" referred to was not only not in anybody's mind at the time, but it was not even physically in existence. Thus both telepathy and clairvoyance were excluded. This left, of course, the possibility of precognition; but these tests were in vogue before the time when precognition was taken seriously as a kind of ESP that the medium might use. The newspaper tests would certainly not any longer be regarded as adequate to exclude what Professor H. H. Price of Oxford University termed the "This-World-ESP" hypothesis of mediumistic results.

It appears that the more we have learned about the psi capacities of the living the more difficult it has become to get evidence that would point unambiguously to some surviving mind as the source. One bold effort to get around this difficulty was made by Mr. Whately Carington in England in the mid-thirties. He applied a personality test to the medium in her normal state and in the trance state in the hope of finding out whether the control personality was a distinct personal entity, as it claimed to be.

Mr. Carington used a word-association test. He read out slowly a special list of words, and he measured with a stop watch how long it took the medium or the control to answer to each word presented with the first word that flashed into mind. Because each person's life is made up of a unique combination of experiences, words come to have a special significance for every individual. The famous psychologist, the late C. G. Jung, showed years ago that each person will show a characteristic pattern of reaction times in the kind of test described. However, in Mr. Carington's application the test did not make any clear distinction between the medium and her control; in fact, in the case of two out of three mediums studied the evidence tended to show that the normal and trance personalities *were related* in the sense that they were opposites. This finding suggested that the medium, in her trance state, was revealing a different side of her own personality from that which was present in her normal state. If we accept this interpretation, the results do not weaken the force of the evidence for survival from the other studies of mediumship. All we can say is that Mr. Carington was not successful in strengthening the case.

In general, however, we may question whether the personality test applied was sufficiently precise to provide the psychic equivalent of a fingerprint by which a personality could be positively identified. The investigation was an ingenious one, and Mr. Carington deserves credit for having thought of it and tried it out. The results from the third medium did seem to point to an independence between the normal waking self and the trance personality. But the results were only enough to keep the question open. The effort spent in the investigation was a great one extending over three years, and Mr. Carington was discouraged from doing any further work along similar lines. So far, no one else has shown any interest in attempting to improve and extend his approach, but the course of research is largely unpredictable, and this work could yet inspire efforts along similar lines and bear fruit. If science is ever to make a definite contribution to the age-old question of the destiny of man beyond death, the search for productive methods must go on, and no one should say that Carington's work was one approach that need not have been explored.

Another new kind of test for survival was one proposed by Dr. Thouless in 1948. As background, I should mention that it had been a fairly common practice among members of the S.P.R. to leave a sealed message in the care of the society. The member who prepared such a message intended to keep its contents secret during his lifetime and to try to communicate what it was after his death as evidence of his continued existence. Dr. Thouless observed that this type of test suffered from two basic defects. In the first place, a medium might learn the contents of the sealed message directly by clairvoyance instead of getting the information from the surviving mind of the person who prepared the test. In the second place, each such sealed message was good for only one trial. Once a message received through a medium seemed impressive enough to justify opening the packet, that was the only time the test could be used. That one time would be enough, of course, if the medium's identification of the sealed message proved to be accurate; but if it did not, there was no way that the test could be repeated. Finally, it was difficult to evaluate the results since it was not easy to decide how much credit to give for a description of the sealed message that was only partially correct.

Dr. Thouless' method also involves preparing a message which he will attempt to reveal after his death. Instead of sealing the message in an opaque packet, however, he has concealed it in what he considers to be an unbreakable code, and the message has actually been published in this encoded form. The point of doing this was to challenge investigators to attempt to break the code with the aid of mediums while Dr. Thouless was still alive, when he had no intention of helping them to do so!

After his death, Dr. Thouless, in case he finds himself surviving with the necessary command of his memory and other faculties, will try to communicate through a medium the key needed to break the code. He will not need to give the message itself, but only the key by which the message can be read. Any number of false keys that mediums may offer will be easily recognized as such because they will not make any sense of the encoded message and thus they will obviously not be the one that Dr. Thouless intends to give. Thus failures before his death strengthen the test (inasmuch as they help to show that mediums did not have access to the key by ordinary ESP); and even repeated failures after his death will not spoil it. The test will remain intact as long as investigators and mediums wish to try to get the correct answer.

Again, the idea is novel and ingenious. There are differences of opinion among parapsychologists regarding just how relevant the results would be as evidence for survival even if the code is successfully broken and the message is revealed. It is easy to think of reasons why a positive result could not be considered as conclusive proof of survival. Mediums are generally strongly committed to a belief that the personality lives on after the death of the body, so it is conceivable that one of them might try to support this belief by unconsciously receiving the key from Dr. Thouless by telepathy while he is still alive and not revealing it until after his death so as to give the impression that the test had succeeded. Or someone might succeed in breaking the code normally by working at it with enough patience and skill and then offer the key after Dr. Thouless' death as if it had been obtained through a medium, or even as if he himself had got it from Dr. Thouless in a dream. Nor can we exclude the possibility that the medium might get the key from Dr. Thouless after his death, not from his surviving mind, but from his mind as it existed while he was still alive. Even though he does not want anyone to get the key from him while he is still living and this may prevent them from doing so, may his *intention* to reveal it after his death not make his present memory of the key available then even though his mind does not survive?

This last-mentioned method would be by ordinary ESP of the kind that parapsychologists refer to as *retrocognition*. It would be ESP working backward through time, as precognition is ESP working forward through time. We do not say much about retrocognition because no one has been able to think of a way that it can be experimentally tested to exclude other forms of ESP. But this is not to say that it can be overlooked as a possible alternative interpretation to survival for a successful outcome of Dr. Thouless' test.

But to recognize the shortcomings of a new method is not to say that it has no value. In the face of a problem that involves so much of the unknown, scientists may only be able to grope their way forward by many faltering steps before they achieve a method that clearly marks the way in which they should advance with bold strides.

Still another line of work pursued in the investigation of mediumship has been concerned with developing better methods of evaluation of the kind of verbal material typically obtained in a sitting. To get an idea of the kinds of practical questions that had to be recognized and overcome in achieving an adequate method of objective evaluation, we cannot do better than cite a section from a typical mediumistic record. This I will do after explaining the situation leading up to the holding of the sitting.

In 1926, Mrs. John F. Thomas of Detroit died. Mr. Thomas' bereavement was so great that a friend urged him to go to a medium. He did so, and the results were so impressive that he decided to continue. In April 1927, when Mr. Thomas went with a stenographer, Mrs. Muriel Hankey, to a sitting with the English medium, Mrs. Osborne Leonard, the message coming through (presumably from his wife) urged him to get in touch with Professor McDougall to arrange for the continuation of his research into mediumship under university auspices. This was the beginning of the steps that led to Mr. Thomas' enrolling in his fifties as a graduate student in psychology at Duke University.

The sitting from which the following section of the record is quoted took place later, in April 1930. Mrs. Hankey was alone with Mrs. Leonard on that occasion, and the medium was not told in advance for whom the sitting was to be held. It lasted from 6:30 to 8:00 P.M., and the verbatim stenographic record filled several pages. As usual, it was concerned with personal statements given by Feda, the entity that represented itself as a little girl who had once lived on earth and that regularly took charge during the trance as Mrs. Leonard's "control." The statements made by Feda were offered as if they were coming from the person who wanted to communicate, in this instance, presumably, Mrs. Thomas.

When Mr. Thomas received the record in America, he broke it down into separate points and marked these as correct, incorrect, inconclusive, and unverifiable for his own circumstances. The record from the particular sitting in question seemed to be largely concerned with a house where the Thomases had lived, and one part of it contained the following statements: "The cupboard wasn't in the middle of the room, you know, like in the middle of the wall, like you put a thing like a wardrobe. It was rather in a corner of the room, because I see her walking along the wall till she came to like the corner. Were they in a room then—I am feeling a room and I feel that directly you open the door of a room you are on steps. It is very funny. You see, you don't often get steps right out of a room, but I feel steps going right up to the door of this room. This is a room they were very happy in, too, and I feel also one part of this place you would be awfully careful in hitting your head. Buddy used to hit his head. Buddy used to knock his head against something that seemed to be rather low. I think he did it more than once because I get a feeling of him saying, 'Oh, juppity—juppity—juppity,' as if to say, 'I have done it again.'"

This particular passage Mr. Thomas broke down into eight items of information, all of which he found to be true for himself. The question is: What value does his analysis have as evidence? May not Mr. Thomas simply have been overly eager to find in the material evidence that his wife was still surviving? Or might not descriptions of this sort be so general that anyone could find ways of fitting the statements to his own personal circumstances or reasons for not doing so, according to whether his personal inclination was toward or against the acceptance of the possibility of mediumistic communications?

Mr. Thomas, in his own research, attempted to deal with such questions by submitting typical items from his large collection of material to other men who were of his age and of the same general status in life. Then the number of items which he had judged to be correct for his personal circumstances was compared statistically with the average number that the members of this similar group marked as correct for themselves. Mr. Thomas' level of accuracy was so much higher that there was no

question but that something more than chance was involved. Was this something extra which he found in the
records, in fitting them to himself, really to be credited
to the powers of the mediums, or could it still be explained as a failure of his method of evaluation to eliminate subjective errors of judgment?

This work was deemed worthy of a Ph.D., and Duke
University awarded Dr. Thomas this degree in June
1933. The general conclusion he reached in his research,
however, was only that the records involved ESP. No
claim was made that the source of this information was
the surviving mind of Mrs. Thomas.

Even so, the method Dr. Thomas used for the evaluation of the material in his thesis left one important
question unanswered which might reasonably be raised
as relevant for his limited, ESP conclusion. How could
one be sure that he was not excessively generous in
marking the material because he knew that the mediums had produced the statements in sittings which
he arranged in the hope of getting communications from
his wife? Since he did his work it has become standard
procedure in such research not to let the sitters know
when they are marking material intended for them. This
is accomplished by having several people take part in
the investigation, but none of them are allowed to be
present in the room with the medium when she is in
trance and producing the records. The accounts received
are identified by code numbers and the material is item-
ized and prepared for marking. Each participant scores
all of the material, his own as well as that of all of the
others, without knowing which is which. Each person

thus must give or withhold credit for each item of information on the basis of what the medium actually said. In this way no one's judgment can be influenced by his wish either to believe or to disbelieve.

Once the records have been marked in this objective manner, statistical tests are applied to see whether, on the average, the participants gave more credit for accuracy to their own records than to those belonging to the others which they also had to score. Unfortunately, by the time we had come to appreciate what was required for an adequate evaluation of the verbal material of mediumship, the emphasis in parapsychological research had swung away from this particular line of study. However, at the present time we appear to be witnessing a renewal of interest in the survival question. Whether this will bring us back to an emphasis upon working with mediums or whether it will make use of other avenues described in this chapter or still others yet to be discovered remains to be seen.

If we have given considerable attention to the investigations of mediumship, this is only as it should be in view of the relatively large place that this problem occupies in the history of parapsychology. But we need to remember that the phenomena associated with the trance state of the medium are, after all, only the products of one particular category of unusual experiences. May there not be other states of mind which are shared by a larger number of people which would occasionally give rise to experiences bearing upon the question of whether the mind survives death? Assuming that our loved ones survive and that they remain interested in affairs on earth and would like to communicate with those they have left behind, may there not be, at least occasionally, times when this could be done without a medium? We have already seen in this book how psi experiences occur spontaneously and fairly frequently in everyday life. Do these sometimes appear to involve communications from someone "on the other side" who might have a special need to send back a message?

All the years of collecting spontaneous psi cases have yielded many instances in which a communication from a deceased individual appeared to be involved. When we begin critically to examine such cases, however, to see whether an explanation is possible solely in terms of the psi capacities of the living, we find few which will stand up against this interpretation. But we should not be interested solely in whether there is, at the present time, any conclusive proof of survival. Rather, we may ask how forcefully the question is raised by the best evidence that is available. We must consider evidence even if it falls short of being conclusive. Examining the better evidence for what it is worth, the investigator must decide whether the situation justifies any hope of an ultimate solution if it is pursued further. Considered in this light, the following cases from non-mediumistic sources are valuable parts of the present picture.

In January 1888 a man living in St. Louis wrote to the American Society for Psychical Research as follows:

. . . In 1867 my only sister, a young lady of eighteen years, died suddenly of cholera in St. Louis, Mo. My attachment for her was very strong, and the blow a severe one to me. A year or so after her death the writer became a commercial traveller, and it was in 1876, while on one of my Western trips, that the event occurred. I had "drummed" the city of St. Joseph, Mo., and had gone to my room at the Pacific House to send in my orders, which were unusually large ones, so that I was in a very happy frame of mind indeed. My thoughts, of course, were about these orders, knowing how pleased my house would be at my success. I had not been thinking of my late sister, or in any manner reflecting on the past. The hour was high noon, and the sun was shining cheerfully into my room. While busily smoking a cigar and writing out my orders, I suddenly became conscious that someone was sitting on my left, with one arm resting on the table. Quick as a flash I turned and distinctly saw the form of my dead sister, and for a brief second or so looked her squarely in the face; and so sure was I that it was she, that I sprang forward in delight, calling her by name, and, as I did so, the apparition instantly vanished. Naturally I was startled and dumbfounded, almost doubting my senses; but the cigar in my mouth, and pen in hand, with the ink still moist on my letter, satisfied myself I had not been dreaming and was wide awake. I was near enough to touch her, had it been a physical possibility, and noted her features, expression, and details of dress, etc. She appeared as if alive. Her eyes looked kindly and perfectly natural into mine. Her skin was so life-like that I could see the glow of moisture on its surface, and, on the whole, there was no change in her appearance, otherwise than when alive.

Now comes the most remarkable *confirmation* of my statement, which cannot be doubted by those who know what I state actually occurred. This visitation, or whatever you may call it, so impressed me that I took the next train home, and in the presence of my parents and others I related what had occurred. My father, a man of rare good sense and very practical, was inclined to ridicule me, as he saw how earnestly I believed what I stated; but he, too, was amazed when later on I told them of a bright red line or *scratch* on the right hand side of my sister's face, which I distinctly had seen. When I mentioned this my mother rose trembling to her feet and nearly fainted away, and as soon as she sufficiently recovered her self-possession, with tears streaming down her face, she exclaimed that I had indeed seen my sister, as no living mortal but herself was aware of that scratch, which she had accidentally made while doing some little act of kindness after my sister's death. She said she well remembered how pained she was to think she should have, unintentionally, marred the features of her dead daughter, and that unknown to all, how she had carefully obliterated all traces of the slight scratch with the aid of powder, etc., and that she had never mentioned it to a human being from that day to this. In proof, neither my father nor any of our family had detected it, and positively were unaware of the incident, yet *I saw the scratch as bright as if just made.* So strangely impressed was my mother, that even after she had retired to rest she got up and dressed, came to me and told me *she knew* at least that I had seen my sister. A few weeks later my mother died, happy in her belief she would rejoin her favorite daughter in a better world.

The above letter and other correspondence and discussion bearing upon the case were published in the *Journal* of the S.P.R. in London. The writer of the letter was identified in the printed account only as Mr. F.G., but Dr. Richard Hodgson, an experienced professional investigator of psi phenomena, visited him in St. Louis and found that the account stood up under close questioning. Mr. F. W. H. Myers, in a commentary on the case, pointed out the obvious interpretation that the sister's appearance represented her awareness of her mother's approaching death and that it was a means of getting her brother to return home before their mother died. Mr. Myers was compelled, however, to point out that Mr. Podmore, another member of the S.P.R., thought that the apparition seen by Mr. F.G. could have been only a projection from the mother's mind.

Today, we would have to consider that far-reaching psi capacities have to be recognized as a part of the normal endowment of the living. These ESP and PK abilities make it all the more difficult for us to feel full confidence in the interpretation that the sister's surviving mind was the source of her apparitional appearance. Granting, as we must, that lifelike hallucinations do occasionally occur, and granting also that the brother could have supplied all of the details involved in his experience from memory and from his own ESP, we *could* dismiss the case as of no interest from the point of view of the survival problem. Yes, we *could;* but if we are going to take a truly scientific position we need not and we should not dismiss it. Rather, we should keep it in mind for what it may be worth, along with all the related material we can find, that might help us to plan and carry through further research on the problem of survival. These thoughts also apply to the following account from the literature of psychical research, the Chaffin Will Case.

James L. Chaffin, a farmer in Davie County, North Carolina, had four sons. In 1905 he made a will, formally witnessed and signed, in which he left his farm to his third son, Marshall. No provision was made for the other members of his family.

In 1921 Mr. Chaffin suffered a fatal fall.

In June 1925 the second son, James P. Chaffin, began to have vivid dreams in which he saw his father standing at his bedside. The events that followed are best described in this son's own words as given in a sworn statement that was taken down by Mr. Johnson, a lawyer and a member of the S.P.R. who visited the family in 1927 to interview them about their unusual experience.

> In all my life I never heard my father mention having made a later will than the one dated in 1905. I think it was in June of 1925 that I began to have very vivid dreams that my father appeared to me at my bedside but made no verbal communication. Some time later, I think it was the latter part of June, 1925, he appeared at my bedside again, dressed as I had often seen him dressed in life, wearing a black overcoat which I knew to be his own coat. This time my father's spirit spoke to me, he took hold of his overcoat this way and pulled it back and said, "You will find my will in my overcoat pocket," and then disappeared. The next morning I arose fully convinced that my father's spirit had visited me for the purpose of explaining some mistake. I went to mother's and sought for the overcoat but found that

it was gone. Mother stated that she had given the overcoat to my brother John who lives in Yadkin County about twenty miles northwest of my home. I think it was on the 6th of July, which was on Monday following the events stated in the last paragraph, I went to my brother's home in Yadkin County and found the coat. On examination of the inside pocket I found that the lining had been sewed together. I immediately cut the stitches and found a little roll of paper tied with a string which was in my father's handwriting and contained only the following words: "Read the 27th chapter of Genesis in my daddie's old Bible."

At this point I was so convinced that the mystery was to be cleared up I was unwilling to go to mother's home to examine the old Bible without the presence of a witness and I induced a neighbor, Mr. Thos. Blackwelder, to accompany me, also my daughter and Mr. Blackwelder's daughter were present. Arriving at mother's home we had a considerable search before we found the old Bible. At last we did find it in the top drawer in an upstairs room. The book was so dilapidated that when we took it out it fell into three pieces. Mr. Blackwelder picked up the portion containing the Book of Genesis and turned the leaves until he came to the 27th chapter of Genesis and there we found two leaves folded together, the left hand page folded to the right and the right hand page folded to the left forming a pocket and in this pocket Mr. Blackwelder found the will. . . .

The paper that they found was in the father's handwriting and it read as follows:

After reading the 27th chapter of Genesis, I, James L. Chaffin, do make my last will and testament, and here it is. I want, after giving my body a decent burial, my little property to be equally divided between my four children, if they are living at my death, both personal and real estate divided equal if not living, give share to their children. And if she is living, you all must take care of your mammy. Now this is my last will and testament. Witness my hand and seal. James L. Chaffin, This *January* 16, 1919.

The twenty-seventh chapter of Genesis recounts how Jacob, the younger brother, supplanted Esau in winning his birthright.

A holographic will is legally valid under the laws of the state of North Carolina.

By the time the second will was found, the son who had inherited the farm under the former one had died and the property had passed to his widow and minor son. The other three sons brought a suit against them to recover their share of the estate. A number of witnesses were prepared to swear that the second will was written entirely in James L. Chaffin's handwriting. On the day of the trial, when the court recessed for lunch after the selection and swearing of the jury, the widow of Marshall Chaffin and her son were shown the second will for the first time. They immediately admitted that the document had been prepared by the father, and they withdrew their objections to having it certified by the court as his valid will.

So much for the essential facts. Now what can we make of them?

A good discussion of the case is given in connection with a review of it which appeared in the *Proceedings* of the S.P.R. in November 1927. There the possibility of an outright fraud, such as would be required for the faking and planting of the second will, is considered. This seemed then, and still seems, a remote possibility. Not only were a number of people, including those who stood to lose heavily financially by so doing, prepared to say that the second will was genuine. Even if by some clever manipulation the will itself could have been forged, it is scarcely conceivable that such a complicated way would have been devised to bring it to light. It would have been sufficient simply to hide the will in the old Bible and then manage to "find" it at the right time. The paper sewed in the old coat and the fantastic series of dreams were not only not of any help; they only introduced a strange element into the proceedings which might have queered the whole game.

Beyond the question of outright fraud, however, what are the possibilities of interpretation? The most obvious one is that the second son, James P. Chaffin, had somehow learned from his father about the second will and that he had forgotten about it until the memory was dramatized in dream form and thus brought back into consciousness. On this point the discussion in the S.P.R. *Proceedings* is so good that it should be quoted:

Mr. Johnson in his statement suggests, only to dismiss, another possible explanation. "I endeavoured with all my skill and ability by cross-examination and otherwise to induce some admission that possibly there was a subconscious knowledge of the Will in the Old Bible, or of the paper in the coat pocket, that was brought to the fore by the dream: but I utterly failed to shake their faith. The answer was a quiet: 'Nay: such an explanation is impossible. We never heard of the existence of the will till the visitation from my father's spirit.'" Clearly, they none of them had any conscious recollection, at the date of the Testator's death, of any mention of a second will, or they would not have allowed the first will to be proved without opposition. Nor was it a matter which, if once mentioned, they were likely to forget, during the short period which intervened between the making of the second will (January, 1919) and the Testator's death (September, 1921). The hypothesis therefore of the "exterioralization" in the form of a vision, of knowledge normally acquired by Mr. J. P. Chaffin, but only remembered subconsciously, is open to grave objection.

We may, I think, at least say that the dream of James P. Chaffin involved ESP, inasmuch as it apparently brought him knowledge about the second will that he could not reasonably be supposed to have obtained through his senses. (Observe that even this conservative conclusion is stated with caution. One could not say that this evidence, if it stood alone, would be sufficient to establish ESP as a scientific fact. But given the vast amount of evidence for ESP from experiments and other sources, it is proper to consider this case as another example of the use of psi abilities.) Can we go further and say that the source of the ESP knowledge obtained in the dream was the surviving mind or the troubled conscience of the father? Here we come once more to the crucial issue, and once more we must frankly admit that we cannot give a clear affirmative answer.

On the face of the matter, the experience looks like an instance in which the father returned in the son's dreams for the purpose of righting a wrong to his family. But where a question of such momentous importance is at issue, we dare not claim an affirmative answer until there is no alternative explanation. The will *was there*, all the while, in the Bible; and the paper giving the clue was in existence in the lining of the old coat. If we assume that the son was concerned with the matter of the injustice of his father's earlier will, he had sufficient reason to want to discover the later document which would set things right. It is not difficult, therefore, to suppose that ordinary ESP (clairvoyance) could have detected the existence of the paper in the father's coat.

We are once again faced with the dilemma from which there is, so far, no way of escape. If we recognize that an individual has access to information beyond his senses through his psi capacities, we simply cannot say conclusively that we have a genuine instance of communication from the surviving consciousness of a deceased person simply because the information appeared to come from that source. Beyond a doubt, this is one of those times when, scientifically speaking, we have no choice but to suspend judgment and go on working.

What direction should further work on the problem take? In part, this question can better be appreciated if we look more closely at the way in which the status of the survival question has changed over the past thirty years.

When Dr. and Mrs. Rhine first decided to enter the field of parapsychology in 1926, both public and scientific interest in survival research was at a high pitch. Resigning their positions as instructors in botany at the University of West Virginia, they went to Boston to spend a year at Harvard and with Dr. Walter Franklin Prince of the Boston Society for Psychic Research. The medium, Margery, was then in her heyday in that city, and the Rhines went to one of her séances. Afterward they made a statement based upon their observations that was unfavorable to her claims, and they found themselves suddenly propelled into the limelight of bitter controversy and big headlines. Thus these two pioneers who had been attracted to psychical research primarily by their interest in the survival question served notice that they were going to adhere to high standards of evidence in their research and let the chips fall where they would.

After the interim year at Harvard the Rhines came to Durham, North Carolina, on a private appointment from Mr. Thomas to assist him in getting his mediumistic material in shape for his Ph.D. thesis. It is interesting to notice in passing that his thesis was submitted twice. The first time, in 1932, Mr. Thomas offered his work as a contribution to knowledge because of the evidence provided for survival. His committee rejected the work as not justifying such a strong position on that problem. The following year, when Mr. Thomas submitted his work the second time, it was accepted; but he had, as we have already seen, toned down his conclusions to evidence for ESP obtained through a number of trance mediums.

When Dr. Rhine plunged into his experiments on ESP in the early thirties, he thought of his work as primarily doing the necessary groundwork for coming back later in a more crucial way to research on the survival problem. He had decided that it would not be possible to come to grips with the survival question until more was known about psi in the living. As things turned out, this pursuit of more knowledge about psi has turned out to be a much longer-drawn-out job than anyone could have foreseen at the time. In the first place, as the work has grown the findings have proliferated and ramified and raised new questions to a much greater extent than could have been predicted at the start. In the second place, the task of learning what we need to know about psi in the living has proved to be much more difficult than anyone could have anticipated in 1930.

As Dr. Rhine himself has repeatedly pointed out, the work on ESP and PK react upon the research on the survival problem in two ways. First, it makes it harder to conceive of the kind of evidence that would be required to provide a conclusive answer to the question. Secondly and conversely, the more we learn about the range and variety of what the normal person is capable of doing through the use of his psi capacities, the more we come to appreciate the existence in man of precisely those qualities that make the concept of survival acceptable as a theoretical possibility. So it is a matter of the survival hypothesis facing difficulties either way: without evidence for psi in the living, we would have no sure knowledge that there is anything about man that could survive death; with psi in the living, we can conceive of survival

but it becomes more difficult to know how to prove that
any seeming evidence for it is not merely a dramatiza-
tion of psi information to suggest communication from
the dead.

In the face of this situation, there are two distinct ways
in which the research worker in parapsychology might react toward the survival question. He might take the conservative approach and suggest that we leave it alone until we know as much as we can find out about psi in
living organisms. This would amount to putting the
question on the table for the indefinite future. Or he
might say that there is much that can be done about the
survival problem right now, and that investigators who
have the opportunity and feel so inclined should devote
their efforts to this question. There are, of course, an infinite variety of positions intermediate between these two
extremes.

The voice of reason and wisdom would appear to say
that no one view should prevail. We need to keep in
mind the overpowering fact that the great, all-encom-
passing objective of parapsychology is the discovery of
the nature of mind wherever it is to be found in the universe. Our major concern may rightly be said to be the
nature, place, and destiny of the personality of the normal, living human being. But the mention of destiny
leads us inevitably to a concern about what happens to
man's mind at the moment of death. We would do well
to consider that this question, with which man has felt
deep concern during all the centuries since at least the
beginning of recorded history, is not likely to prove to
have been only an idle query. Rather, it is one that de-

serves whatever amount of scientific attention may be required to find the true answer—an answer so clear that it will be universally recognized and accepted as established knowledge. From such research all men stand to gain; from its neglect, only those will benefit who have a vested interest in protecting their own personal and intellectual commitments against having the floodlights of scientific inquiry illuminate this area where the present obscurity only marks the existence of an uneasy truce between the dread of the hereafter and the solace of faith.

8

Do Animals Have ESP?

The truly scientific person is one who is able to look beyond the boundaries of present knowledge. He must observe with an open, receptive mind the unknowns that he sees there but be able to suspend judgment about what it is that Nature is trying to tell us. Most important of all, when he finds things he cannot explain he must *not* dismiss them as mere trivia. Is not the truly scientific person, in short, the one who refrains from thinking that the outer boundaries of knowledge have already been established, but who recognizes, instead, that there may still be some real surprises in store for us as new discoveries are made?

Whether or not an individual makes his living as a scientist is not the point. Millions of people who pursue non-scientific careers, as well as millions of housewives and students, are genuinely qualified as scientific thinkers, while thousands of professional scientists are, alas, not. Consider, for example, your own reaction when presented with the following items of unprocessed information tossed our way by Nature. How do you stand on this test of scientific aptitude?

Item: A parapsychologist on the staff of the Duke laboratory brought a cat fifteen miles from its home to add it to an experimental colony of animals he was using for ESP tests. The cat was hauled in a box in the car. The minute the box was opened at the end of the trip the cat jumped out and disappeared in the direction of home. The next day it was back there and the parapsychologist got word to come get it again.

Item: A neighbor told me that he wanted to get rid of a dog, so he took it five miles away through the city of Durham, North Carolina, and turned it loose in a thickly populated section where he thought someone would be glad to claim it. When the owner got back home the dog was in the yard waiting for him. (This display of loyalty in the animal made him, he said, a faithful master.)

Item: When the time arrives in the autumn for the annual migration of birds from their Northern breeding grounds to their wintering areas in the Southern Hemisphere, in some species the *young* birds that have never before made the journey travel separately from the old ones. In some instances the young ones go first, yet they reach the right place thousands of miles away and are there when the experienced fliers arrive.

Item: Several years ago a family named Doolen moved from Aurora, Illinois, which is about forty miles west of Chicago, to Lansing, Michigan, about a hundred and seventy-five miles northeast of Chicago. Before leaving Aurora the Doolens gave away their pet dog, Tony. Six weeks later Tony found his master on a sidewalk in downtown Lansing. From the dog's behavior, its recognition of the fact that it had come to the end of its long search was instantaneous and complete. The master, on the other hand, could hardly believe his eyes; but all doubt was removed when Mr. Doolen found that Tony was still wearing a special collar which was too large and in which he had cut an odd-shaped hole for the buckle. The dog had very distinctive markings and it was recognized by all the four members of the Doolen family as well as by visitors from Aurora who had raised it as a puppy. The distance the dog would have had to travel would have been greater than the two hundred and fifteen miles indicated, since it would have had to go southward to get around Lake Michigan. In fact, the dog wore tags from Jackson County, directly south of the one in which Lansing is located, so Tony had apparently stopped there long enough to be adopted and to find that he did not like it. Incidentally, there was never any doubt about the fact that the reunion with the Doolens was the end of the journey!

Item: I heard the mother of a family in New Jersey tell about how their pet dog suddenly went under the house and started a whining, continuous crying. That was the only time the dog had ever acted in this way, and they were not able to call him out or get him to stop his strange barking. Later in the day news came that the older son of the family had been killed in an automobile accident on the way home from college, and the time of his death coincided with the beginning of the dog's unusual behavior.

Item: A scientist friend told me that he once had a pet cat that would go and wait just inside the door several minutes before he reached home. He said that the members of the family came to know that the cat's behavior meant that he would be home within a few minutes, and that this did not depend upon his coming at the usual time.

Item: A fellow parapsychologist said that his wife, as a little girl, had a pigeon for a pet. She remembered that the pigeon had a way of finding her wherever she might be. This happened so often and under such circumstances that it did not seem possible that the pigeon was locating its owner by sight or any other ordinary sensory means. In other words, the surprising feat could only be explained by those who observed the behavior as ESP.

Item: A twelve-year-old boy in West Virginia found a homing pigeon which had a permanent, seamless aluminum band on its leg with the identifying number 167. The boy kept the pigeon as a pet. Later the boy was taken to a hospital that was seventy miles, as the pigeon flies, from home. After he had been there for a few days he told the nurse one night, when there was a snowstorm raging outside, that she should open the window for a pigeon that was trying to get in. The nurse did it to humor the boy. He instantly recognized his pet bird and told the nurse to look for the number 167 on the band. It was there. When the parents later visited their son they were surprised to see the pigeon. They were sure it could not have followed the car when the boy was first brought to the hospital, since they had taken care of it at home after that.

Item: Mrs. Martin Johnson of Lund, Sweden, reported the following case to the staff of the Duke Parapsychology Laboratory. A few years ago, in a public school where she was a teacher, a magpie flew in through an open window of a corridor during a recess period and perched on the shoulder of a boy in a group of about forty pupils. The boy immediately exclaimed: "It's our summer bird!" His family had spent the summer in a cottage about fifty miles away, where they had acquired a magpie which they kept as a pet. When they moved back to the city they left the magpie behind. It was so clear that the bird that flew in the window knew the pupil that his teacher excused him from school so he could take it home. In this instance not only did the bird trail its owner such a great distance that chance can hardly be the explanation, but the animal picked out its human friend in a large group of children and by so doing made its own identification certain.

Item: From the number of cases that have been collected on the topic, there is reason to take seriously the observation that dogs do sometimes find the graves in which their masters have recently been buried. Faithful to their owners in death as they were in life, these pet animals take up their lonely vigils without regard for their own needs for either food or water.

This test for scientific thinking could be extended to fill an entire book, but the foregoing items must serve the present need for illustrating some of the unexplained observations in the world of animal behavior by which Nature invites our attention. What is your own reaction? Did you reject the foregoing accounts as old wives' tales, or as the products of overworked imagination in younger persons, or even as evidence of faulty memory in presumably scientific people? Or did you, on the contrary, find yourself uncritically accepting item after item as a statement of simple fact? Neither reaction earns a passing mark as the scientific one to take toward such claims. Yet these and other such reports do have a place of high value *in that they raise questions*. And new questions *must* be raised if we are to escape a feeling of complacency with the stage of knowledge we have already reached. Such complacency leads to stagnation, and stagnation in turn leads to decay. From such examples of what animals have done when there was no conceivable sensory basis for their behavior we come, then, to the question of whether they may have been using ESP. If, in addition to recognizing the question raised by these anecdotal cases, we acquire at the same time the motivation to seek the answer through research, we have passed our test with the highest possible mark.

So we have our question—Do animals have ESP?— but the answer is not to be taken for granted until the findings are clear through research. To underscore this necessity, let me describe briefly an instance in which the mysterious way-finding ability of a species was finally solved in terms of a remarkable combination of sensory abilities. This is the discovery by the German zoologist, Professor Karl von Frisch, of how bees are able to find their way from the hive to a distant source of nectar or pollen and back again. This will serve as a good object lesson against allowing a mere mystery to cause us to leap to the assumption that there *must* be something beyond the operation of the senses (that is, ESP) *always* just waiting to be discovered.

In 1951, Dr. Rhine and I, together with two scientific colleagues whose paths had been temporarily joined with ours in a special research project, made a trip to Europe. Our mission was to visit laboratories where work was being done that was, directly or indirectly, relevant to the question of whether animals have ESP. One individual we planned to see was Professor von Frisch in Munich. Before our trip I had made a special study of his research, and I was therefore asked to take charge of this interview. Professor von Frisch had, after twenty years of patient and persistent effort, finally broken a secret code by which bees have been communicating with one another for untold ages. Here we need to concern ourselves only with the main outlines of his great discovery.

The fact that bees "make a beeline" from the hive to the source of food and back to the hive is common knowledge. Beekeepers have also long known that, when one bee discovers a new source of supply, other worker bees in the hive are soon flying out in vast numbers to help collect the treasure. It seemed obvious that the bee that made the original discovery had some way of telling the others in the hive where to go and what to look for. But how? This was the problem upon which Professor von Frisch worked for so long with agonizingly slow progress. At the end of the twenty years the final answer came with amazing swiftness.

As a scientific investigator, Professor von Frisch did not simply sit and admire his busy bees or work with the hives in the manner of an ordinary practical bee-keeper. Rather, he established feeding stations so that he could control the distance and direction of the food source from the hive. Also he provided sugar water having a distinctive flavor and odor for the bees. Then he put observation windows in the walls of the hive so he could peek at what was taking place inside.

At first, what he saw in his role as Peeping Tom did not make sense. A bee returning for the first time from a newly discovered source of food simply seemed to be dancing for joy on the vertical wall of the honeycomb. Yet the bees that were watching this wild dance would shortly afterward leave and go straight to the feeding station from which No. 1 had returned. The dance seemed to have something to do with the fact that the first bee could tell the others where to go. But what?

When Professor von Frisch and his colleagues finally got the answer they were seeking, it turned out that there was not just *one* kind of dance but *two*. A successful scout bee that had something to tell about food at a *greater* distance—say between one hundred yards and three miles from the hive—used one type of dance to get its message across, whereas a scout that found food near the hive danced in quite another way. It was largely because the investigators had assumed that there was only one answer to the question they were putting to the bees that the human sleuths had so much trouble making sense of what they saw. When they finally overcame this false way of thinking and realized that the bees had two ways of communicating for the two different distances, the whole stereotyped game of bee charades began to make sense.

First, let us learn the language of the bees as regards the dance for a distant source of food. There are three things the scout bee has to tell his fellow workers: what kind of food source has been discovered, which way it is, and how far.

The way in which the dancer reveals the kind of flower was the easiest part of the puzzle to solve. The returning scout not only brings a load of nectar or pollen; it carries also the odor of the flowers where it has made its haul. The bees in the hive who want to get the message pick up this part of it by the use of the well-known senses, chiefly odor and taste. So the worker bees that are eager to go know *what* they should find on their foraging trip, but how do they know the direction in which they should fly?

Which *way* to go the scout communicates to those in the hive by a dance which it performs in a straight line on the wall of the comb. During the dance along this line, the dancer waggles its abdomen, presumably to attract attention. The direction in which the bee itself advances while doing this dance is related to the direction of the food source from the hive. If the direction of motion is vertical, this means that the other bees should fly directly *toward* the sun; if the direction of travel is straight down, this means they should fly directly *away* from the sun. Motion horizontally to the right means, Fly at a right angle to the sun, keeping it on the left-hand side; while motion horizontally to the left means the opposite. Similarly, a dance done on some diagonal line on the wall of the comb is interpreted by the bees as meaning that the direction to the food forms the same angle with the sun as the line taken by the dancer forms with the vertical direction on the comb. So now we see how the bees learn which *way* to go, but how do they know *how far?*

Since the space in which the dancer can work is limited, it is necessary for it to return again and again to the starting point. In so doing, the dancer, when it reaches the end of the line, makes a half circle in order to get back to the beginning before resuming its waggle dance along the significant straightaway. This return path is not a part of the dance itself and it is made sometimes to the right and sometimes to the left. As a result, what the bee does is tracing out loops which touch each other on the meaningful, common boundary by which the right-hand and left-hand circles are joined. Thus the actions performed during the dance show the bee tracing out time after time a squat figure 8.

The distance is inversely related to the time the bee takes to complete a full loop of the dance. When the food source is nearby but not nearer than approximately a hundred yards, the dancing bee steps along rapidly, completing each full turn in the shortest time possible. But when the new happy hunting ground is out at the maximum range at which the bees are capable of working, the dancer goes through his paces in slow motion. If we may translate this difference in timing from bee language into English, we might render the fast dance as saying: "Quick, fellows, it's right there over the first hill and you can be back here in almost no time at all!"

while the slow dance is saying: "It's *that* way, but be prepared to fly to the edge of the world to find it, and it'll be a time before we'll be bumping into you back here again." Dances done at some intermediate rate reflect discoveries of food supplies at intermediate distances on this same general scale.

What about the second kind of dance, the one for food found closer than half a mile? A returning scout having such a message to relate moves about on the wall of the comb while waggling its abdomen, *but without dancing in any particular direction*. In English, the meaning of this random dance would appear to be: "It's right outside, willing workers! All you have to do is go and look yourselves, and you are bound to find it!"

After the above description of the dance of the bees was written, recent findings showing that there is more to the story came to my attention. *Time* reported in the May 31, 1963, issue that Dr. Harald Esch of the University of Munich had taken the further step of placing a small microphone inside the hive. When he listened as well as looked, he discovered that the bees were "talking" to one another by distinctive sounds during the dance. The scout bee that was doing the dance made a drumming sound, the length of which was related to the distance to the food source, and the bees that were following made short "beep" replies. This further discovery does not, of course, cancel out anything that Professor von Frisch discovered; it only adds an important further dimension to his findings.

That, in its barest outline, is the story of Professor von Frisch's remarkable breakthrough in discovering how scout bees tell others in the hive what to do. There are other details of the story that cannot be told here, but those interested in pursuing the topic will be able to do so in Professor von Frisch's book included in the reading list at the back of this one. Also, if any of you care to go further along these lines, you will discover that his work has opened up a whole new field of knowledge of how other insects and even creatures of other kinds similarly orient themselves in terms of the position of the sun through their perception of polarized light.

As explained earlier, the bee story was introduced here as an illustration of the fact that mere ignorance of the explanation of an event in the realm of behavior is not enough to say that it is a psi phenomenon. But the coin also has a reverse side. The fact that one particular mystery was cleared up by finding a sensory explanation is no excuse for neglecting the important question raised by some of the remaining examples of unexplained animal behavior—the question of whether animals may have ESP.

That the use of this excuse may be a real danger seemed to be indicated by something that happened at the symposium on ESP which the Ciba Foundation held in London in May 1955. Twelve people—mostly parapsychologists—were invited to give papers on assigned topics, and twelve English scientists were invited to observe and to discuss the papers. One of the observers was Dr. C. G. Butler of the Bee Department, Rothamsted Experimental Station, England. Following a paper in which I raised the question of whether ESP might be the key to the age-old puzzle of pigeon homing (as discussed in the next chapter), Dr. Butler was asked to tell how a sensory basis for bee orientation was now known. He did so, which was all right. But the manner in which the topic was introduced and handled seemed to carry the implication that if the problem of bee communication, which had been a mystery for such a long time, was finally reduced to sensory terms, might we not safely assume that all similar questions would likewise someday be so explained?

Whether or not that was the intention—and I hope I was mistaken—there can be no doubt that this is the assumption which governs the attitude and actions of the vast majority of scientists. But we dare not be guided by this or any other constrictive principle applied as brakes to research into new areas. To do so is to make today the error which is so easy to see in our predecessors in the history of science but which is so difficult to recognize in ourselves. That is, we simply cannot afford to place a penalty upon those who elect to be unorthodox in research. Therefore, even though the research should, unlikely as it now appears, in the long run prove that only man has psi abilities, the research on the question of whether animals have ESP must nevertheless be done.

The title of this chapter, "Do Animals Have ESP?" was put in question form as the only appropriate one to use. As a query, it reflects the unfinished stage of the research on this problem. We are dealing here with a topic which is still very much in the forefront of research, not at the point of reaching a definite conclusion. Therefore it will be sufficient if we deal only briefly with the experiments which have been conducted to try to find out if animals do have ESP.

Because one aspect of this research is being carried out on a broader front, both biological and parapsychological, it is more complex than the rest. This work —the pigeon homing research—will therefore be reserved for separate treatment in the following chapter. In the remainder of this one, we will be concerned with five separate ESP experiments made with four-footed animals: one study done with a horse; two experiments with dogs; and two with cats.

Chronologically, the first animal experiment was one made with dogs, animals that had been trained for a circus performance based upon the carrying out of unspoken commands. This work was done in Russia. It dates from the period just before World War I until several years thereafter. (Four years ago we learned that this work marked only the beginning of an active interest in ESP at the University of Leningrad. It continued very actively for twenty years, then the research halted but the interest itself persisted and finally resulted in the establishment of an official laboratory for the investigation of these problems—see Chapter 10.)

The leader in the Russian dog investigations was the famous brain physiologist, Bechterev. An opportunity to undertake some experiments with the trained dogs was presented when their trainer, Durov, gave a performance in Leningrad (then St. Petersburg). After the show Durov sought out Bechterev, whom he had recognized in the audience, and asked his co-operation in some research with the dogs. In the first tests, the dogs carried out complicated tasks in Bechterev's own apartment when Durov gave the silent commands.

After the war further tests were carried out in Moscow, where Durov had his headquarters. Twice Bechterev himself was present, and twice he sent one or two of his associates. In these further tests the task which the dog was asked to do—such as going to the side of the room where it was to jump upon a chair and reach up and paw a portrait on the wall—were often known only to Bechterev himself. In later tests, Durov himself was completely absent and the experimenter who knew what the task was and who gave the silent command was completely shielded from the dog's view. Yet there was such success that Bechterev published a report of the work. In it he reached the conclusion that the thoughts of the persons involved had somehow directly (that is, without the use of the senses) influenced the behavior of the dogs.

In 1927, only a few months after Dr. and Mrs. Rhine had come with Professor McDougall to Duke University, the three of them decided to take a trip to Richmond, Virginia, to see the young horse, Lady. The owner, Mrs. C. D. Fonda, had trained the horse, then a year-old filly, to spell out the answers to questions by using her nose to point out letters and numbers on a special apparatus. The fame of the horse spread rapidly, and long afterward I heard Dr. Rhine comment that at the time of his visit to see Lady he had not yet found his bearings at Duke in research with human subjects. Therefore the challenge of a visit to see the horse seemed relatively greater then than it would have even a few years later.

In fact, the investigators made two visits, a year apart. The first year they were successful in winning the owner's confidence and getting her to withdraw from the test situation. Under these conditions, Lady gave strong evidence of ESP when one of the investigators chose a test question and carefully guarded against the possibility of giving Lady any cues while the other two visitors worked with the horse and took down the answers. The findings were written up and published with tentative conclusions that the horse had demonstrated parapsychic abilities.

On the second visit, the situation seemed quite different. The research workers observed that Mrs. Fonda seemed to need much closer control over the horse than she had the year before, and efforts to get further results that were free of possible sensory guidance were of no avail. As a result of the second visit the Rhines published a second report in which they admitted failure to find any further evidence of ESP, but they saw no reason to change the conclusions reached in the former article.

So Lady won her laurels in the pages of science. She held the attention of active investigators relatively briefly. She continued for many years, however, to be a tourist attraction at her stand just south of Richmond, and many were those who came and who went away professing that they had seen and believed.

The two experimental investigations of ESP in cats were carried out by Dr. Karlis Osis in the Parapsychology Laboratory in the early fifties (the second one in collaboration with Mrs. Esther Foster). In the first study, the test was one in which the animal had to choose between two equally attractive food pans. The experimenter, screened from the cat's sight, decided on some random basis which should be the "correct" pan for each trial. Then he concentrated upon having the cat make the same choice. In the more crucial trials, two experimenters worked together. One of them prepared the pans and handled the cat and the other, behind a screen, merely selected the target and concentrated upon the desired choice. The results were not spectacular, but they were good enough for the experimenter to say that the cats had been influenced on *some* psi basis to make more correct choices than could reasonably be attributed to chance. However, he could not say whether the success depended upon the ESP abilities of the *cats* or upon some essential psi element which the *experimenter* was contributing to the man-cat relationship.

In the second cat experiment, an effort was made to point up more definitely the ESP-in-cats interpretation. This time, neither of the two experimenters knew which was the correct choice. Two food pans were used, but only one of them contained a bit of food. It was, in other words, a test for clairvoyance.

To make sure that there was no sensory cue from the odor of the food, a special apparatus was made to provide an artificial breeze blowing from the cat toward the two pans. This would, of course, carry any odors away in a neutral direction.

This investigation did not give such high results as the earlier one, but the results were nevertheless significant in certain striking and consistent ways. The investigators concluded that once again the cats had given significant evidence of ESP. Under the conditions of the experiment the results did appear to be dependent upon the cat. But was this a necessary conclusion? This is a question to which we can more profitably return after the animal study still to be described, the second experimental one reported thus far with the dog as subject.

Early in the fifties we began to get news clippings in the Parapsychology Laboratory at Duke about the amazing feats of Chris, a pet dog in the home of Mr. G. H. Wood of Warwick, Rhode Island. Chris was reported to be able to answer any kind of question put to him. The dog gave the answers by pawing at his master's forearm. In most of the performances, both public and private, Mr. Wood knew the answers to the questions. However, those who observed the action could not detect any sensory cue by which he might be telling the dog when to stop pawing.

Chris's feats, if correctly reported, were not all easy to attribute to guidance by sensory cues. Mr. Wood himself seemed sincere in his interest and genuinely desirous of having Chris studied scientifically. Certainly it did not seem justifiable to classify the case as a clever act of man-dog magic. By proper scientific thinking, the matter could not be so lightly dismissed. It therefore seemed worth while to attempt a firsthand investigation in spite of the handicap of distance.

Mr. Wood was approached by the laboratory in 1954 to see if he would be interested in trying some tests with Chris along more objective lines. The idea was welcomed, and Chris was taught to call ESP cards by pawing once for circle, twice for cross, three times for wavy lines, four times for square, and five times for star. Mr. Wood soon reported that Chris was calling cards which were known to the person conducting the test (making telepathy a possible interpretation) with a level of success approaching a hundred per cent correct choices.

It was not until the fall of 1957, however, that a representative of the laboratory went to Rhode Island for the first time to see Chris in action. The investigator was Dr. Remi J. Cadoret. He had recently joined the research staff, coming from Yale (where he had taken his M.D.) via a two-year period in the Air Force Medical Corps.

Dr. Cadoret made two trips to Rhode Island during the fall and one in January 1958. He improved the experimental conditions in two ways: one was by getting Mr. Wood to test for clairvoyance in the work he did alone; the other was to carry out clairvoyance tests in which Dr. Cadoret himself was a second observer.

The former tests yielded highly significant results. For example, one experiment with the cards in opaque envelopes was planned in advance to include five hundred trials with ESP cards. Where 100 hits would be the most probable chance score, the actual number of hits was 152. The chance odds against getting a score as high as this purely by luck are more than 1,000,000 to 1. Beyond all reasonable doubt, when Mr. Wood alone worked with Chris remarkable results were forthcoming.

On the other hand, clairvoyance tests carried out in Dr. Cadoret's presence gave results that were of the psimissing type. The number of hits were so consistently below the expected chance average that they would have been expected to happen by pure luck only 12 times in 1000 such tests. This bordered upon being proof of ESP by being so consistently below the chance level.

After the January 1958 visit, Dr. Cadoret told me that he was going to help Mr. Wood to write up a joint research report, then he wanted to get out of the dog ESP business. This left an opening which I was glad to try to fill, and the first visit to Seaford a few weeks later to investigate the Herrmann household disturbances provided a convenient opportunity for me to visit the Woods and see Chris in action.

Like the hundreds before me who had seen Chris put through his paces, I was impressed with his performance in answering questions put to him. With what seemed like studied indifference—yet with a seasoned trooper's dependence upon his spectators and with his eyes turning frequently toward the tasty food from which he had come to expect a morsel after each correct answer—he would paw out his responses on Mr. Wood's outstretched arm. There were also a few other people with whom Chris could work successfully. The questions could be about anything—What is my name? How many grandchildren do I have? When is my wife's birthday?—as long as Mr. Wood knew the answer.

Sometimes, I was informed, Chris had given correct answers to questions when no one present knew what they were. These exceptional instances included giving the score of a baseball game before it was announced publicly and pawing the guilty parties in an unsolved crime.

If Mr. Wood was cuing the dog, it was certainly done very subtly. To my knowledge, no one ever claimed to know how Mr. Wood could be doing so. But this is not to say that the idea of cues could be dismissed. In fact, as long as Mr. Wood knew the answer to the question put to Chris, it was necessary not only to recognize the possibility of sensory explanation, but to give it preference over the ESP hypothesis.

The card tests introduced by Dr. Cadoret had got past the stage at which Mr. Wood consciously knew the answer. In the clairvoyance condition, no one knew the target. However, it is conceivable that Mr. Wood himself was the ESP subject. He could have been getting the card by clairvoyance and giving Chris a subtle sensory cue to get him to give back the answer that Mr. Wood already had by ESP.

Indeed, this possible interpretation was taken seriously, and Mr. Wood began testing himself with the cards to see how well he could do when he consciously took the role of subject. In all these tests, carried out at irregular intervals over a period of many months, the results were consistently at the chance level. But one can always suppose that Mr. Wood did not *want* to succeed in these self-tests, since this would have cast doubt upon his belief that Chris was responsible for his own spectacular results. In spite of the experimenter's failure when testing himself with the cards, it is still conceivable that working with Chris was merely a psychological foil, *the* ideal test for Mr. Wood himself as an ESP subject.

I got along well with Mr. and Mrs. Wood, with Chris,

and with the friends who were actively interested in the investigation. But none of us could get anything but chance results while I was there. The only positive accomplishment during my first visit was the consideration given to the testing procedure that should be followed after my departure. We agreed that the "general extrasensory perception" procedure (making either telepathy or clairvoyance possible) could be used provided the agent who was looking at the cards was in another room out of sight of Mr. Wood and Chris. The agent should always shuffle and cut the pack of cards after going to his station. Then the agent would only speak once to indicate when he was ready to turn up the first card and look at it. After that, Mr. Wood would ask Chris to paw his "call" for the first card and the choice would be recorded in a bound notebook. Then Mr. Wood would say, "Next," the agent immediately would turn up the second card, Chris would paw his answer for it, and Mr. Wood would record the call. Then there would be the ready signal for the third card, and so on until the run of twenty-five was completed.

At that point the agent would bring the cards back into the room where Mr. Wood and Chris were waiting. The agent would observe while Mr. Wood recorded the order of the targets alongside the calls and scored the hits.

I paid a second and final visit to the Woods in July 1958. I learned then that the above procedure had been giving remarkably successful results. The run scores were mostly in the teens, where 5 is the expected chance average. The chance odds for all the results combined were billions of billions of billions to one. The chance hypothesis was clearly out the window; genuine success was obviously achieved in these tests on some basis or other.

In planning his work the psi investigator must be willing to face and deal with every conceivable alternative to the parapsychological interpretation of significant findings, including the possibility that he might be deceiving himself by wishfully making errors to make the results agree with his hypothesis. He must also be willing to entertain the idea that an assistant may be fudging in the test to please the experimenter.

In the two-room procedure described above, there was no possibility of motivated errors on Mr. Wood's part. When he recorded the calls, he did not know the order of the targets. The possibility of errors in his recording of the targets and checking of the hits was slight because this part of the procedure was observed by the agent. Furthermore, these tests were done with the standard ESP pack in which there are exactly five cards of each of the five symbols. If there had been any error in the recording of the targets, this would be easily detected from the fact that the card record did not show a five-times-five balance for that run.

But the above two-room ESP procedure left something to be desired as regards safeguarding against conscious effort by the agent to "help things along." The dog's pawing on Mr. Wood's arm made a noise, and the agent knew the code by which the different symbols were indicated. All that an overly zealous agent would need to do, therefore, would be to count the number of paws given on any trial and then pick out a card that would match the call. This interpretation injects the nasty possibility of conscious cheating, of course; but those of us who have been seriously involved in the psi revolution have learned from experience that some people are so skeptical about ESP that they will not hesitate to advance fraud as the explanation to avoid having to accept ESP as a fact.

The kind of procedure needed was one in which it would not be possible for anyone involved in the test to make any motivated error, consciously or unconsciously, without the full knowledge of the other. Thus the error would be caught and corrected; or else it would be necessary that at least two people should have agreed to falsify the results. When the safeguarding precautions are such that the only alternative to ESP is the hypothesis of deliberate collusion to falsify the results, this is as far as it is feasible to carry experimental controls in psi research—and it is further than research workers in other branches of science go!

The plan I proposed, which Mr. Wood quickly accepted and which we put into practice, was this: I had numbered ESP packs prepared at Duke. First, the identifying numbers were placed on the outside of the boxes in which the cards came from the manufacturer. Then each pack was thoroughly shuffled and the order of the cards was recorded on a record sheet under the identifying number of the pack. The cards were then put back into their box. The records of the cards were filed away at Duke and the numbered packs were sent to Mr. Wood, who kept them in his own possession.

When a pack was needed for an ESP test with Chris, Mr. Wood took one of the boxes, recorded its number at the top of the column for the run in his record book, and handed the cards, still in their box, to the agent.

The agent left the cards in the box until he reached his station in another room. Then he removed the cards from the container and *cut the pack*. He was told not to shuffle them in any way, but to make a simple cut by dividing the stack into two parts and putting it back together so as to reverse the positions of the two sections of the pack. After the cut, the agent said "Ready" and then turned up the first card. From that point the run proceeded in the usual manner.

What did this procedure accomplish? The agent could not do anything with the order of the cards even if he could hear what Chris was pawing for each trial. This was impossible because the order was already on record at Duke. Mr. Wood could not gain anything by looking at the cards in the box before handing them to the agent. Since the agent was instructed to cut the pack, any illicit prior knowledge would have been useless for getting hits on the order that would exist *after* the cut. The record of the cards at Duke eliminated the possibility of motivated errors in the recording of the cards.

When Mr. Wood sent a copy of the calls with the hits marked to me at the laboratory, I could quickly find out where the cuts had been made and verify the results.

After this plan was agreed upon in July 1958, I returned to Duke and soon thereafter sent Mr. Wood a supply of shuffled packs in numbered boxes. Months went by with no report from Rhode Island. This was not surprising since Chris had been chronically ill when I left there. But finally, in 1960, I received the call records of a number of runs that had been carried out from time to time as opportunities were found. The scores were so high as to be quite obviously beyond the range of merely lucky coincidence. But in case you are interested in why this statement is true in the statistical sense, the next paragraph deals with the mathematics of chance odds for high run scores in a general, non-technical way. If you prefer not to go into this just now, you can skip ahead and take up the main story again in the next paragraph.

The expected chance score on a run is, of course, 5. In a large number of runs in which only chance factors are present, as when one randomly shuffled ESP pack is checked against another, the score expected most frequently when this process is done many, many times is also 5. As we go away from this score on the scale toward either higher or lower scores, the expected frequency of occurrence of such a score drops down gradually. For the interpretation of the results of these Chris tests, we were interested in how often we would find, by chance alone, run scores in the higher ranges. The following table shows how often chance results alone would, on the average, yield a particular run score *or a higher one*. (In such an evaluation, we should take into account not only the odds for the particular score obtained, but at the same time we must add in the odds for all the higher scores, up to and including the odds for a perfect run of 25 hits. This I have already done in the following table.)

Run Score	Expected by Chance	
11 or more	1 in 150 runs	
12 or more	1 in 500 "	
13 or more	1 in 1,960 "	
14 or more	1 in 8,300 "	
15 or more	1 in 41,500 "	
16 or more	1 in 200,000 "	
17 or more	1 in 1,400,000 "	
18 or more	1 in 10,000,000 "	
19 or more	1 in 100,000,000 "	
20 or more	1 in 10,000,000,000 "	

With this table as a general guide, we will be able to appreciate how remarkable the run scores obtained with Chris on the Duke numbered packs really are. The runs themselves were spread over a year, from October 1958 to October 1959. Only one run—rarely two—was done at a time at widely and irregularly spaced intervals which depended upon how Chris felt.

The principal agent was Miss Rosemary Goulding, a friend who was strongly devoted to Chris and to the investigation of his unusual abilities. When Miss Goulding was in one room and Mr. Wood worked with Chris in another room, the run scores were 13, 15, 11, 16, 13, 16, 16, 18, and 14. When Miss Goulding was in her home in Providence and Mr. Wood and Chris were at home and the tests were done over the telephone, two runs gave scores of 16 and 19.

When these two experimenters reversed roles, Mr. Wood looking at the cards and Miss Goulding taking down Chris's calls, runs made between two rooms gave scores of 14, 4, 10, 6, 14, 7, 3, 11, 4, 20, and 11. Here we have evidence of large swings between significant high scoring (14, 10, 14, 11, 20, and 11) and runs that were so near the chance average that they give no indication of ESP (4, 6, 7, 3, and 4). Yet taking these eleven runs as a whole, the total score is 104 where 55 is the most likely chance score. A score of 104 or more in eleven runs would be expected to happen by chance only once in more than 100,000,000,000 such series. This means we *must* dismiss the chance explanation. This result, incidentally, will give some idea of how much more significant the scores were when Miss Goulding was the agent, when *all* the runs gave high scores, as shown in the preceding paragraph.

On two other occasions Mr. Wood was with Chris and a different friend was in another room with the cards. The scores were only slightly above the chance level: 6 and 9. These runs and those with the low scores when Miss Goulding managed Chris are reassuring in that they show that there was not something about the test that automatically produced high scores. Apparently the *psychological* conditions had to be favorable in some subtle way, and the drop in scores occurred regardless of whether Mr. Wood was working with Chris or Miss Goulding was doing so.

The fact that high scores were obtained by two different people working with Chris makes it look more as though the dog were responsible for the results rather than his handler. But it would take many more people working successfully in this role to prove that the animal was the one demonstrating ESP.

In the face of these results, what are the alternatives to the ESP explanation? I see only two that are conceivable, and they are hardly within the bounds of reason.

One is the possibility that the successful agents were unconsciously giving sensory information of what the cards were to the person working with Chris. The two experimenters were around the corner during a run and out of sight of each other, but the connecting doors were left open and therefore the situation was not a sound-proof one. It is easy to see that some method of signaling by sound could have been used if they had wished to develop a trick for the amusement of spectators. But usually there were no spectators; and any *conscious* signaling would have required deliberate collusion, which is, as I have already said, out of bounds as a proper scientific consideration. This leaves only the possibility that the agent had slipped unintentionally into the use of some sound code which the experimenter had learned to detect and interpret. This is all too farfetched to take seriously for the two-room ESP tests. (At first glance, the telephone tests might look like a better control against sound cues than those in different rooms, but it is doubtful if that position is defensible. It might well be easier to detect such slight sounds as whispers or changes in breathing over the phone than from one room to another.)

The other alternative interpretation is that the people concerned in the tests made some honest mistake in interpreting the rules they were supposed to follow and thus nullified the safeguards. The worst that can be said about these results is that they were not obtained by professional research scientists who were especially trained and widely experienced in testing for psi abilities. This conceivable interpretation, like that of sensory cues, does not rob the series of its value as evidence of ESP. Rather, it only means that the findings must be regarded with a degree of tentativeness.

Speaking reservedly, I consider that these results present a strong challenge to the trained psi research worker to investigate further along similar lines when he finds the opportunity to do so. Unfortunately the opportunity for further work with Chris is gone. I received a letter from Mr. Wood stating that Chris died in February 1963, at the ripe old canine age of fourteen years.

And so we have the results of five published experimental tests for ESP in animals and the details regarding some hitherto unpublished results with Chris. Add to these the indications given by the anecdotal case material of unexplained direction-finding and other kinds of behavior in which a sensory explanation cannot be given. Do they yet amount to proof that animals have ESP? At this stage the answer must be no. The reason is not that the experimental results were not clearly significant nor the conditions adequately safeguarded. Rather, the reason is that it is not yet possible to ascribe the *experimental* results definitely to the animal subjects rather than to the human participants in the tests.

We have to allow for the possibility that the human experimenter might be using his own ESP (where that would be necessary) and that he might be influencing the animal's choice by one means or another, including the possibility of his exerting a PK influence upon some part of the animal's organism or nervous system. Does this mean that it is hopeless to think that sufficiently definite proof that animals have ESP can ever be found? No, certainly not! On this particular sector of the battle line, the fight for new and clear answers has barely begun. The experimental studies are clearly worth while even though it will be difficult to make them definitive.

Perhaps in the long run more real progress toward getting to the crux of the problem will be made by studying the forms of unexplained behavior suggesting that animals use ESP under natural conditions. When a pet cat travels hundreds of miles to rejoin its family who have gone ahead to a new location where the animal has never been before, and when most of the cat's journey is made after all the human beings concerned about the animal have long since given it up as lost or dead, it is difficult to conceive of any possible psi involvement of the owners in the animal's finding of the new home. And pigeons must have had at least a rudimentary homing ability before man existed. If further research should establish that ESP is the basis of one or both of these classes of behavior, it would be superfluous to inject a human explanation for something that the animals so obviously do under natural conditions on their own.

Of two things we can be sure at the present stage. One is that the bringing of the research on the question of ESP in animals to a successful conclusion will not be easy. The other is that the achievement of the goal will be eminently worth while, whatever the cost.

9

Winged Messengers, What Is Your Secret?

How do birds guide their flight when migrating over distances of thousands of miles? How are they able to return home when taken hundreds of miles into strange territory? The long-distance migratory flights that occur in nature and the shorter homing flights which man, whether for pleasure, profit, or scientific purposes, exacts from his feathered friends have puzzled observers for centuries. Of speculation about the answers there has been no shortage, but most of the suggestions have been sheer guesses, lacking the kind of careful analysis and experimental support that would give any one of them the status of an acceptable scientific hypothesis.

But during the past two decades there has been a growing interest among scientists in the problem of bird orientation. Over an even longer period of years, the practice of banding migratory birds has resulted in great strides toward establishing the amazing facts regarding the pattern and precision of seasonal movements of different species. But when we want to solve the general problem of *how* birds find their way, their ability to return home when they are taken only a relatively short distance into strange territory offers a more attractive prospect for experiments.

Migration and homing may or may not, in the long run, prove to be the same thing. That remains for research to decide. But the big experimental push of the past twenty years has been made on the homing question, and particularly in studies of the homing pigeon. We may profitably and properly, therefore, confine attention in the present chapter to experiments on pigeon homing.

From ancient times the pigeon has been famous for its homing ability. Birds of this species are easily domesticated provided they are left alone to enjoy themselves in a suitable loft. Until recent years homing pigeons were widely used for carrying messages, and until 1956 the U. S. Army Signal Corps kept pigeons for this purpose. These birds were trained to home to mobile lofts, and, given three days' notice, the Signal Corps pigeoneers could set up lofts in strategic locations for the maintenance of communications under conditions requiring radio silence, as when agents are dropped by parachute in enemy territory or when ships are on advance patrol. Also, history records some memorable occasions when enterprising newspaper reporters and businessmen called upon these winged messengers to help them get the jump on their competitors. Nowadays, however, pigeons are used primarily for the sport of homing races.

Man's discovery of the pigeon's homing ability and his use of it for his own practical advantage or pleasure has not miraculously brought understanding of the bird's secret of how it is able to find its way. In fact, the answer still eludes even the research workers who are studying pigeon homing. For many years it appeared that this problem was shunned as one that presented a mystery too great for science to tackle. But the research of the past two decades shows that the scientists have finally staked out their claim to a problem area that had previously been largely left to the attention of pigeon fanciers, nature lovers, and poets. Already, much has been learned about the pigeon's homing ability, discoveries which advance us toward the final answer. In the process much has been accomplished in the way of ruling out hypotheses of which their promulgators had become enamored to the degree of mistakenly offering them as *the* solution.

About 1950 scientific attention to the problem of pigeon homing was broadened to include the possibility that something beyond strictly physical or sensory principles might be involved. In other words the question was explicitly raised in the Duke Parapsychology Laboratory whether the explanation might lie at least partly in the area of ESP. The difficulties of zoologists in finding an explanation in non-ESP terms fully justified our asking whether their failure might not be due to their closing their eyes to the basic principle. We considered it worth while not only to raise this issue but also to do something about it. We decided to launch a research program aimed at testing whether pigeons home by

ESP. It seemed to me that this problem presented a strong challenge for the psi research worker, and I welcomed the opportunity to tackle it. This chapter is the story of the past dozen years as they relate to that decision.

When Dr. Rhine and I, together with two colleagues, were in Europe in 1951, one person we especially wished to see was Dr. Gustav Kramer in the Max Planck Institute in Wilhelmshaven, Germany. Dr. Kramer had done experiments in which he proved that birds keep on a course, as in migratory flights, by taking account of the position of the sun. He and his co-workers had even shown that birds allow for changes in the sun's position during the day. Thus the direction of flight remains the same even though the sun itself shifts. Obviously, here was a clue which might be important for the solution of the homing puzzle.

This work of Dr. Kramer's had quickly earned for him a world-wide scientific reputation, but his discovery was concerned only with how birds hold to a flight course after the direction itself has been determined. It did not deal with the more advanced problem of how a pigeon, for example, may be able to *choose* the correct home direction in the first place. When we arrived in Wilhelmshaven we found that Dr. Kramer and his colleagues had gone on to this new question and that they too were planning research with homing pigeons. Dr. Kramer himself had serious doubts at the start as to whether the pigeon is capable of homing without the benefit of previous training by many flights in the required direction.

Simultaneously, a young zoologist at Cambridge University, Dr. G. V. T. Matthews, had been doing pigeon homing experiments for his Ph.D. research. He not only doubted that pigeons have any genuine homing ability, but he also expected to earn his degree by clearly *proving* this point. He ended up with his degree for proving the reverse.

Thus we see how skeptical scientists were as recently as a dozen years ago regarding pigeon homing. This skepticism prevailed in spite of the fact that the ability of the bird to find its way had been recognized for centuries. In modern times special strains have been developed that are cherished for their speed and reliability in returning to the loft, and thousands of people who are fascinated by the pigeon's uncanny ability have established lofts and organized clubs devoted solely to holding homing races. Today there are hundreds of thousands of pigeon fanciers throughout the world. In Belgium, for example, pigeon racing has become the most popular national sport. The fanciers marvel at the bird's homing ability and they speculate about its nature. However, they are, generally speaking, not concerned to study the problem scientifically. They are content to improve the homing ability of their flocks by selective breeding from the most successful homers while continuing to live with their mystery.

Yet, in spite of all this, most scientists seriously doubted as recently as 1950 that pigeons had any *inborn* homing ability. Could not everything that they were able to do be explained on the basis of their being trained to fly in the direction that the pigeon fanciers knew in advance would be used in their races? (Indeed, fanciers do follow the practice of releasing the birds on the prearranged flight path, starting first at a short distance from the loft and gradually increasing the distance.) Or if young pigeons do occasionally return from a great distance the first time they are taken away from home, may they not simply have followed older birds who already knew the way?

Dr. Matthews trained pigeons from his loft in Cambridge to return from the north. He made a number of releases at increasing distances up to approximately a hundred miles in that direction. Then he took these same birds eighty miles west of Cambridge and released them one at a time, watching through field glasses each one go out of sight. He expected the birds to fly off to the south, but instead they clearly preferred the east, the direction toward home. Again, the same birds were taken eighty miles south, and from here they flew north toward home, instead of south as they had been trained to do. Dr. Matthews, by hindsight, thought that the long period of training had been necessary for bringing out the homing ability; but once the ability was awakened in the birds by the long training, they were able to return home from any direction. The question was: *How* did the birds know which way to fly to get home?

One old idea that Dr. Matthews tested was the kinesthetic hypothesis. This was the view that the pigeons could somehow register every twist and turn of the outward journey, every acceleration and deceleration of their motion, even though they were hauled in covered boxes. When the pigeons were released, this inner registration would let them know which way to go to get back home. Dr. Matthews divided his birds into two groups. Those of one group were transported in the usual way, while the others were rotated throughout the journey. The members of the second group should have had an incomparably more difficult task in keeping track of where they were being taken, yet they showed as much homing ability as the group hauled in the ordinary way. This appeared to dispose of the kinesthetic hypothesis, or at least to make it so unlikely as an explanation of homing that the research workers were turned away from it until other conceivable explanations were more fully explored.

When we were in Wilhelmshaven, Dr. Kramer and his group were preparing pigeons for their first real homing experiment. They planned to make releases from two hundred miles to the south without previously training the birds to home from another direction. Instead they gave their pigeons short releases from different directions at distances of ten miles from the loft simply to get them accustomed to being handled.

After Dr. Rhine and I returned to Duke, we received the news that the pigeons had performed beautifully in the 200-mile release. Every group had vanished north toward Wilhelmshaven, and many of the pigeons completed the 200-mile flight within a few hours. Most of them had homed before the end of the first day. Even those pigeons which gave up and entered a strange loft were apparently not really lost. The birds carried message bands requesting that the finder report the time and place to the research workers, and the majority of the reports came from lofts which were on or close to the line between the release point and Wilhelmshaven.

Clearly, both the work of Dr. Matthews in Cambridge and that of Dr. Kramer and his associates in Wilhelmshaven showed that pigeon homing poses a real problem for science. The battle was joined to see who would make the great discovery.

As a matter of fact, during the forties a major effort to establish the basis of homing had already taken place in the research of Dr. H. L. Yeagley, a physicist on the faculty of Pennsylvania State University. Dr. Yeagley had developed, purely on a speculative basis, a hypothesis that pigeons are able to home because they are sensitive to two physical factors: one, the earth's magnetic field; and the other, a force associated with the rotation of the earth, known as the coriolis force. Each of these physical forces covers the entire earth in a "field" which varies in intensity depending upon the distance from the center. For the magnetic force, the center is the Magnetic Pole, while the field of the coriolis force is centered on the North Pole. Since the North Pole and the Magnetic Pole are at different places, the coriolis and magnetic fields do not coincide, but they cut across one another with varying intensity and different angles of their lines of force. This makes it possible to define any spot on the earth's surface by its measurements in terms of these two fields, just as any spot has its latitude and longitude definition.

This is all too complex to make clear in such a brief account. But, so far, the hypothesis is in the realm of established physical principles and the facts are beyond dispute. The fancy begins when these things are supposed to be relevant for pigeon homing. Professor Yeagley speculated that pigeons, in flying about the home loft, feel both the magnetic and the coriolis forces. They become accustomed to how these forces feel at home, and this becomes the bird's means of identifying where the loft is located. When the bird is taken away from home, the hypothesis supposes, it does not feel right, and simply flies about until it discovers in which direction it needs to go to bring it once more to the familiar feeling from its magnetic and coriolis senses that characterizes the home territory. Guiding its flight in this way, the pigeon ultimately comes close enough to recognize familiar landmarks, and the final stage of homing depends on the use of the eyes.

Now it so happens that different points on the earth's surface show exactly the same characteristics in so far as the interaction of the magnetic and coriolis fields are concerned. Professor Yeagley found that a spot in Nebraska had the same magnetic-coriolis values as the location of Pennsylvania State University. He therefore approached the Signal Corps at Fort Monmouth, New Jersey, where the Pigeon Center was maintained, with a research proposal for testing his hypothesis. The Signal Corps agreed to support him with pigeons, equipment, and the necessary dollars.

The test consisted, first, of establishing pigeons in mobile lofts at Pennsylvania State University where, presumably, they were kept long enough for them to accept that location as home, sweet home. The birds were then moved, caravan style, to the substitute magnetic-coriolis home in Nebraska. There tests were made by taking the pigeons away from the lofts in the new location and releasing them. The Yeagley hypothesis supposed that they would fly back toward the Nebraska location, since this was the nearer spot which gave the right feel of the magnetic-coriolis forces.

The results were ambiguous. Professor Yeagley claimed that they supported his hypothesis. The experiment was picked up and widely publicized in the daily press and in a feature article in *Life*. So, for millions of people, the pigeon homing problem was solved! But not for the scientists. Not only was the Yeagley experiment rejected on the grounds that it was physically inconceivable and that Dr. Yeagley had tended to overinterpret his data; but when other research workers began actively to investigate the homing problem a few years later, tests in which the birds homed with magnets attached to their wings proved that the earth's magnetic field is not involved. So the homing problem was rescued from this particular one of several premature claims for solution that have marked and marred the history of research on this problem.

After returning from Europe in 1951, I constructed a loft in my back yard and got my first pigeons. The first requirement, of course, was the practical one of learning how to keep the birds alive, well, and happy. The people from whom I acquired stock—mostly members of pigeon racing clubs in nearby cities but also Major Otto Meyer of the Pigeon Center at Fort Monmouth—were all very helpful. Pigeons seemed to thrive under my care.

Then came the stage at which the youngsters were ready for homing tests. I followed the example of pigeon fanciers, which meant that the birds were kept shut up in the loft most of the day and allowed out only for short exercise flights or when they were taken away to be released. My plan was to make releases from all directions beginning at a few yards and gradually working out as far as, say, a hundred miles.

Unfortunately, things did not go well at all. I began losing my birds in large numbers by the time they were being released, during the summer of 1952, only a few miles from the loft.

Meanwhile, news from Germany indicated that the success of the experiment of the preceding year had been repeated with even more phenomenal results. Dr. Kramer and his associates were getting very striking homing from two hundred miles with pigeons that had not previously been more than ten miles from the loft. The great difference between their results and mine pointed clearly to some fundamental difference in our methods of handling pigeons. Dr. Rhine suggested that we should try to get Dr. Kramer over for a month to help me get on the right track.

Dr. Kramer accepted our invitation and arrived early in December 1952. On his way, he had stopped in New York to visit scientific colleagues in his own field, ornithology. They naturally had asked what brought him to America. When he explained that he was here at the invitation of the Duke Parapsychology Laboratory, he got some serious words of warning and advice regarding the consequences of associating with a research center that dared even to raise the question of whether ESP might be involved in pigeon homing. When I met Dr. Kramer at the airport, he seemed to be somewhat more reserved than when we visited him in Wilhelmshaven. Not until later, when we had become fast friends, did he tell me that his colleagues in New York had advised him to be on guard.

Dr. Kramer stayed only one day with me when he first came. He took one look at my loft and made only one suggestion: Open that prison and let the jailbirds fly free. Then he went to Wisconsin to spend the month of December with friends.

When he returned to Duke in early January 1953, I insisted that we should spend our month of collaboration going through an actual experiment, making it as much like the ones that he and his colleagues had done in Wilhelmshaven as possible. He agreed to this plan, even though the birds available were younger than he would have wished to use for a long-distance experiment. Before January was over, we made a release from a fire tower 140 miles from the loft with birds that had earlier that month homed only three times from distances of less than ten miles in three different directions. Our birds homed beautifully. One older hen (nine months) we released singly. She was a bird Dr. Kramer had pointed out in the loft as not a true homing pigeon, and we took her along on the trip only with the expectation of losing her. She covered the 140 miles in four hours and five minutes. The younger birds, averaging approximately four months of age, performed less phenomenally, but more than half of them returned, and of those who failed to do so several were reported as having been found at points close to the home line.

Dr. Kramer was so favorably impressed with the opportunity of conducting pigeon releases in North Carolina even in the winter months that he suggested that I try to obtain a grant for this research. If this could be done, either he himself or a colleague would come over to work with me for a part of each year. In Wilhelmshaven the winter weather was so bad that he had to interrupt the homing experiments.

Accordingly, shortly after Dr. Kramer returned to Germany at the end of January, I sought and got the approval of Dr. Paul Gross of the Duke University administration to submit an official grant request to the Office of Naval Research. This proposal became the basis of a contract between Duke University and ONR which provided funds for the investigations. In return, we promised to do experiments in collaboration with my German zoological colleagues to try to discover the basis of the pigeon's homing ability. The proposal also made clear that the main purpose, as far as the Parapsychology Laboratory was concerned, was to find a satisfactory way of dealing with the question of whether ESP is involved in this behavior.

The objectives were clear, the basis of collaboration was well defined, ONR approved the proposal, and the relationship was to be an altogether happy one from beginning to end. From the start we were personally convinced by the work of Dr. Matthews, the results of the Wilhelmshaven group, the first Duke experiments, and others that pigeons had some secret that was worth any amount of effort to unravel. We also recognized that it might take still more evidence to win general acceptance of this fact, especially if there were no sound explanation for it. We agreed that, until the explanation was known, no conceivable hypothesis should be excluded from consideration. It was clear that the sensory hypotheses that had already been offered, chiefly the kinesthetic hypothesis and the Yeagley hypothesis, had not stood up in experimental tests. Now, Dr. Matthews himself was advancing a new one as the last remaining hope of explanation—the sun navigation hypothesis. (More about this later.)

When Dr. Kramer returned to Duke after the ONR contract went into effect, the laboratory held a dinner in his honor. On this occasion he said that he had no full-fledged hypothesis of homing. Until the evidence pointed in some other direction, he could not object to the ESP hypothesis of the parapsychologists. At least, he went on, our hypothesis was one which we felt we had established as a principle in human behavior. Therefore it was perfectly proper for us to raise the question of whether it might explain pigeon homing. However, as a zoologist, he preferred to explore this behavior further to discover more of the basic facts about it. With enough facts, the correct sensory hypothesis could ultimately be fashioned if, as he thought was likely the case, the final explanation should be found in sensory terms.

Sometimes Dr. Kramer sent over his primary associate of that period, Dr. Ursula von St. Paul. Sometimes their visits overlapped. When one or both of them were present, we worked primarily on general problems, striving

to advance scientific knowledge regarding pigeon homing. However, they did not hesitate to co-operate on the
projects which I initiated in the effort to develop a suitable ESP test of this behavior.

But the *first* collaborator after the ONR project went
into effect was a British colleague whose help was as unexpected as it was welcomed. This was Dr. Robert H.
Thouless of Cambridge University, who came to spend
three months in the Parapsychology Laboratory in the
fall of 1953. Before leaving Cambridge he had talked
with Dr. Matthews about his pigeon homing research
and particularly had discussed with him his new hypothesis that the pigeons locate the position of the release
point by taking account of the time of day and the position and apparent motion of the sun. The Matthews hypothesis assumed that the birds, in the course of their
daily flights about the home loft, observe the sun and
become thoroughly familiar with the precise shape, ele-
vation, and timing of its daily pathway across the sky.
Measured precisely enough, these sun characteristics
uniquely define the general territory of which the loft is
the center. Then the bird is taken under cover and forci-
bly removed from this home region. According to the
sun navigation hypothesis, when the pigeon is finally released many miles away in strange territory, it is momen-
tarily lost. The best it can do is to circle about at the
release point. But this circling period, said Dr. Matthews,
is not wasted. The bird uses the time to observe the sun
and check its characteristics in terms of how the sun
would look at home at that precise moment. When the
bird has had time to appreciate what is wrong with the

sun at the release point, it instinctively chooses that direction of flight which will restore this sky mark to its familiar pathway in the heavens. When the sun looks right again, the bird is near enough home to recognize familiar landmarks and to find the loft by eyesight.

Thus, said Dr. Matthews, the bird is doing with its inborn equipment something which the human navigator is able to do only with the aid of his instruments: the map, the sextant, and the chronometer. What was Dr. Matthews' evidence for this hypothesis? Mainly circumstantial: the observation that birds do not home well in cloudy weather. When the sun is not visible, they tend to vanish at points that, for a large number of flights, are fairly evenly distributed around the circle rather than being grouped in the home direction; they take longer getting home; and with prolonged cloudy weather there are heavier losses. This circumstantial evidence Dr. Matthews attempted to support with a special experiment which yielded ambiguous results. But in the main he argued for the acceptance of his hypothesis because, said he, there was simply no other conceivable way in which homing could be explained. The possibility of an ESP basis he treated with utter scorn.

By the time Dr. Thouless came for his three months at Duke, Dr. Matthews had published several reports on his experiments. Each succeeding one advanced stronger claims for his sun navigation hypothesis, and the idea, like the Yeagley hypothesis before it, was gaining a certain acceptance, particularly in England. I was especially glad, therefore, to have a British scientist, particularly one from Dr. Matthews' own university, join me in ex-

periments to test the idea of whether a period for observation of the sun was necessary before the bird could
choose the home direction.

Our approach was very simple. We divided our pigeons
into two groups, one of which we called the "sun" group
and the other the "no-sun" group. The birds in the former group were exposed to the sun in their cages at the
release point. Those in the no-sun group were kept in the
shadow of an opaque screen until the moment of release.
We made the releases from atop fire towers which provided ideal points for the observation of the departure
flights of the pigeons.

The experiment showed no difference between sun
and no-sun birds. Members of the two groups vanished
from sight with the same speed and their departures
showed the same accuracy of response: a general tendency to vanish in the home direction. Our conclusion
was that a longer viewing of the sun at the release point
was of no consequence in the bird's homing response.

Actually, Dr. Kramer himself had started his pigeon
homing research with a favorable attitude toward the
sun navigation hypothesis. He was interested quite in-
dependently, without knowing that Dr. Matthews was
thinking along similar lines. But Dr. Kramer and his
associates soon abandoned the sun navigation hypothesis
of homing on the basis of their unexpected contrary
experimental findings.

For the first few years of the Duke-ONR project,
therefore, one of our main jobs was to correct the impression that the mystery of pigeon homing had been
solved. We became sure that we had the facts to do the

job. But the question was: How could we make the facts known so they would most quickly become effective?

The answer was found in a suggestion first made by Dr. Gross. In 1954 he said that we should consider holding a conference at Duke on the bird orientation problem.

Early in 1955, I reminded him of this suggestion and said that April of that year, when Dr. Kramer would be over again, would be a good time. Dr. Gross said that it might be worth while for me to approach the National Science Foundation for support. A short time later, I discussed this question with the proper person at NSF in Washington. He told me that it would be a simple matter for them to approve the budget for a conference, but he would like to ask Dr. Donald Griffin, professor of zoology at Harvard and the leading authority in the U.S.A. on bird orientation, if he thought the project was advisable.

A few days later I got the word from NSF. Dr. Griffin's opinion was that this problem needed not a conference but more research.

Meanwhile, a citizen in the Duke community, Mr. Charles E. Ozanne, had become interested, and he pledged up to five thousand dollars to underwrite the expenses. When Dr. Kramer arrived I told him of these developments. He wrote a letter to Dr. W. H. Thorpe, Dr. Matthews' sponsor at Cambridge, asking if the two of them would like to come. We received a cabled reply saying that both of them would attend if their expenses were to be paid. Dr. Kramer then telephoned Dr. Griffin and asked if he and some of his colleagues would want to join us. Without hesitation the answer was yes, even though the delegation from Harvard would, under the circumstances, have to come at its own expense.

We held a small but an intensely concentrated conference. All told, there were fifteen members. In addition to the two Englishmen we brought over and American scientists who had worked on the problem, we had two mathematicians, an astronomer, a Cambridge physicist who was already in the U.S.A., and Major Meyer from the Signal Corps Pigeon Center. We also invited a fancier from a pigeon club in Hawaii that held its races at night.

The conferees heard papers from a number of the participants, but mainly the proceedings shaped up as a debate between Dr. Matthews and Dr. Kramer. Dr. Matthews had come full of confidence. During five years of intensive research he had published a number of papers on his findings. His scientific monograph, soon to be published by the Cambridge University Press, rounded up his own efforts in the field, along with a comprehensive, though deprecatory, glance at the work of others, and boldly stated that his findings established the sun navigation hypothesis of homing.

At the start of the conference, some of the members were leaning toward Matthews' view. But during the debate that went on for two days Dr. Kramer's logical points began to take effect. On the afternoon of the second day the meeting was moved to the planetarium at the University of North Carolina where tough technical questions regarding what the pigeon would have to do to navigate as Dr. Matthews would have us believe were settled on the spot by conjuring up sun paths at will.

Dr. Matthews had gone out on a limb of speculation with his sun navigation hypothesis and by the end of the Duke orientation conference the limb had been sawed off behind him. I find it hard to believe that he did not feel the fall. By majority agreement among the participants, the conference reached no official conclusions and there was to be no publication of findings or of the proceedings as such. In fact, this account is, as far as I know, the only public admission of the fact that we met. There was, it seemed to me, a strange atmosphere of furtiveness about the whole matter, almost as if the fact of our meeting in the shadow of the Parapsychology Laboratory might tarnish the professional image of some of the participants! The opinions expressed here are solely my own, including the opinion that my views are secretly shared by most of the others who were there.

Dr. Matthews and I were already scheduled to hold a further debate on the question just two weeks later. The occasion was a symposium on ESP planned by the Ciba Foundation in London for early May 1955. At that meeting Dr. Matthews was speaking largely to a receptive audience: scientists from his own country who had already been persuaded to favor his hypothesis through his numerous publications. His book was supposed to be the capstone of this phase of his career, since he had already taken up another position in a government research station. In reading his paper, if he had any doubts about his conclusions as a result of the Duke conference, he did not show them. He spoke as if the sun navigation hypothesis was the eagerly awaited answer to the age-old mystery of pigeon homing. Erroneous ideas in science do not expire instantly, but die a lingering, painful death.

My own paper at the Ciba conference offered no conclusions. Rather, it pointed out the requirements for a crucial test of whether ESP is a factor in pigeon homing and outlined some of the efforts to meet these requirements. Even now, eight years later, this line of research is still short of its goal. But since the search for an ESP test of homing is the main plot of the story of the pigeon research as far as the psi revolution is concerned, I must describe these efforts as far as they have gone and outline the prospects for final success.

But before turning to that topic let me mention briefly the main discoveries that have been made *about* homing over the past ten years, discoveries that move us toward the final solution even though they do not as yet give the answer the research worker is seeking.

Pigeons *are* capable of homing from a great distance, even the first time they are taken out of sight of the loft. This natural ability of the pigeon to return from a distance on the first release comes as a complete surprise to thousands of pigeon fanciers who have always considered that it is necessary to train pigeons to home.

One fancier in Richmond, Virginia, Mr. R. R. Grundy, gave me fifteen fledgling birds. Four months later he came down to help in an experiment in which his birds and some of my own were to be taken seventy-five miles on their first release. He entered into the experiment in a spirit of total skepticism: pigeons simply could not know which way to go under those circumstances! Yet as we released our thirty birds, one after the other, and watched almost every one go out of sight in the direction of home, Mr. Grundy's attitude changed completely. He was eager to get back to the loft to see how many of the birds had already arrived. To his surprise (but not to mine!) not one pigeon had arrived when we reached home eight hours after the first birds were released. Half of the birds got back in their own good time, most of them late on the day of their release or during the next forenoon, which is typical for long-distance releases of first-fliers.

Another person, Colonel John B. Cooley of South Carolina, who kept pigeons as a hobby volunteered to raise some birds for us which we could then use for homing experiments there. When Dr. Kramer, Dr. von St. Paul, and I went down for our first experiment, Colonel Cooley asked us what we proposed to do. When we mentioned taking the birds for a fifty-mile release, he was sure that we would lose them. Pigeons just could not home from such distances without training! But to his surprise and delight, half of the birds got home. The next spring he raised more birds for us from pairs mated from the fifty-mile first-fliers of the previous year. These youngsters he offered for our experiments *provided* we would take them fifty miles on the first release! We worked for several years on this plan, and the homing ability of his flock increased phenomenally during this time. Colonel Cooley was happy to be able to offer for sale to other fanciers birds with ancestors that had for several generations homed fifty miles without training!

Homing success may vary from one day to another

even when weather and other known conditions are the same. This unexplained "day" difference was seen in some cases when the same birds were released on two different occasions at the same point. Sometimes the performance on the first release was excellent while that on the later one was very poor even though the conditions of wind, temperature, cloudiness, haziness, and the like seemed to be more favorable on the second day. Here is experimental support for the observation, all too familiar to pigeon fanciers, that on some days pigeon races result in "crashes"—that is, catastrophic losses—even though the weather conditions between the release point and home seem ideal.

The direction in which the bird is displaced from home influences the speed and success of his return. The favored direction for homing may depend upon the region and may vary from loft to loft within the same region. In Wilhelmshaven and in Durham, for example, the best results are obtained when pigeons are taken away to the south. No one yet knows why, but for the pigeon this effect of the direction of home from the release point is real enough.

Birds that have spent their entire lives in a large wire aviary have homed to it when, on the first trip they ever made outside, they were released at distances of up to two hundred miles. But birds raised in an aviary having opaque walls and a wire top so that they were able to observe only the sky showed no tendency to home when they were taken away and released.

The *direction* in which the pigeon flies from the release point is related in a general way (but not in the

sense of Dr. Matthews' hypothesis) to the bird's appreciation of the position of the sun as interpreted in terms
of its appreciation of the approximate time of day. This
has been clearly established by the experiments of Dr.
Klaus Schmidt-Koenig. He began this work in Wilhelmshaven and repeated and extended it after he came
to work at Duke under the original ONR project in the
Parapsychology Laboratory. (In 1959 the project was
transferred to the Zoology Department, where the Duke
bird orientation studies are still continuing.)

Dr. Schmidt-Koenig put pigeons in rooms where the
light was artificially controlled. For a period of several
days the pigeons were subjected to a "day-night" sequence which was six hours out of phase with the natural day. For a control group of birds, other pigeons
were subjected to the same conditions of artificial light
and darkness but without any shifting in time of the day-
night sequence. The objective was to reset the internal
clocks of the experimental birds by six hours but not to
shift the clocks of the controls.

When two groups of birds prepared in these two ways
are taken to a release point, there is, as a rule, a difference
of ninety degrees between the averages of the vanishing
points of the two groups. Those birds that have had
their day shifted have indeed reset their internal clocks.
As a result they misread the position of the natural sun.
The experiment does not tell us how the pigeon knows
where he is in relation to the loft. But it does show that,
once this mysterious insight has taken place, it is translated into a course of flight based upon the sun's position
in terms of the pigeon's time of day. Since a six-hour

shift in time represents one fourth of a full day, the shifted birds take a course that is displaced by 90° or one fourth of the full compass circle. Many of them later correct their error and finally reach home.

One *negative* finding has turned up so consistently that it is worth mentioning. In spite of repeated efforts under a wide variety of conditions, no one has been able to find any reliable evidence of pigeon homing orientation except when the birds are in free flight. To see if the birds will walk home, investigators have clipped their wings or fastened them down with special gloves. The birds have not co-operated! Again, pigeons have been turned loose in the center of a large aviary set up in strange territory. There has been little or no evidence of attempts to escape toward home.

One experimenter, Dr. H. G. Wallraff, in many regular releases in Germany set each bird free in the center of a special cage which had a number of symmetrically arranged exits. He found no tendency to choose one of the exits nearer home.

Another experimenter, Dr. H. B. Hitchcock, of Middlebury College, Vermont, worked one summer at Duke on the ONR project testing birds in a special cage in which the pigeon earned its food as a reward for pecking the "correct" button. Dr. Hitchcock tried to "condition" the bird to respond to the button which was toward the loft (just as the bird apparently responds to the distant home as a goal when it is released for free flight), but his efforts were unsuccessful.

A number of other efforts to study homing without releasing the bird have been tried, and all have been disappointing. It would, of course, be a big advance in method if we could bring pigeon homing into the laboratory for experimental study. But it is of no use to bring the *pigeon* indoors if we leave its homing ability outside. Someday, someone may succeed in this objective on which so many have failed. But until that happy day comes, we will have to study pigeon homing the pigeon's way or not at all.

Against this background of general facts and recent discoveries, you are, I hope, better prepared to see the reasons for the steps already taken and the big one yet to be attempted in the search for a crucial test of whether ESP may be involved in pigeon homing. The essential idea is to set up an experimental situation in which the pigeon may choose between two possible directions, one of which it should take if homing is a sensory function and the other of which it would choose if it is orienting by ESP.

In 1953, I began working with pigeons in a mobile loft. The loft was shifted between two locations that were approximately twenty-five miles apart. The two spots were selected so that there was a fire tower midway between. Thus there was a suitable release point available in case the experiment ever reached the test stage.

Young pigeons were introduced into the loft at four weeks of age, as soon as they could shift for themselves but before they could fly. During the next three months, while they were reaching the earliest suitable age for homing releases, the loft was shifted between the two points at frequent intervals (every two or three days at the start and, later, once a week). The birds had complete freedom while they were at each place to enable them to become fully familiar with their two home territories. The hope was that the birds would adjust equally well to both locations; that they would have no strong preference for either one as such; and that the place where the loft itself happened to be would therefore be the more desirable for the pigeons. If things went according to plan, when the birds were old enough I would take the loft to the release tower at the midway point, remove the birds that were to be tested for ESP homing, take the loft out of range of sight and hearing of the birds and the releaser-observer left at the tower, and decide on some random basis at which of the two places the loft should be parked during the test.

After a suitable lapse of time the pigeons would be released. If their departures showed a sufficiently strong preference for the spot where the loft was located, this would be strongly suggestive evidence for ESP.

Unfortunately, the plan failed because my colleagues and I had not fathomed a basic characteristic of pigeon nature. Before the birds were old enough for releases, they rebelled against having the loft moved from one place to the other each week. Sunday was moving day for me. The morning after I had moved the loft, the pigeons would abandon it and fly back to where they had been during the days just preceding. There they would shift for themselves for two or three days. Only then were they driven by hunger and lack of shelter to return to the loft itself, where they finished up the week. Thus, for the pigeons, moving day usually fell on a Wednesday.

When I came again on Sunday and moved the loft once more, the whole pattern was repeated in reverse. The three or four days they had spent with the loft between *their* moving day and *my* whimsical persecution on the next Sunday were enough to make them want to stay put, regardless of which place was involved.

This whole pantomimic clash of wills showed that pigeons quickly become adjusted to living in a particular place. The attraction of the more recently familiar landmarks was so great that they did not hesitate to abandon the loft rather than accept the unwelcome move. Since we had not foreseen this effect, the experimental plan did not provide any way of dealing with it. Obviously the pigeons would not be capable of making a free choice at the mid-point tower to reflect any pulling power of the loft itself.

Over the next two years I changed the experiment a number of times in search of a way around this difficulty. I tried not letting the birds out of the loft until late in the afternoon, when they would have to come down to roost after a short exercise flight. The loft was opened each day at a place where the birds had never flown before. The first few releases on this plan went off well. Then came the day when the pigeons simply refused to stop exercising and come back to the loft, even though it was plainly within sight. Had the repulsive force of strange landmarks accumulated until it made the familiar loft itself unacceptable?

Then I tried moving the loft to a new place each night

and opening it up so that the pigeons were free to fly about as much as they liked the next day. Under these circumstances, everything seemed to be going well until it became apparent that the number of pigeons in the loft was smaller than at the start. I discovered that some of the birds had abandoned the loft to take up residence at one of the places with which they had become familiar on one of the preceding days. To collect these landmark worshipers I retraced the moves, taking the loft back to the previous locations, one after the other. As soon as the wayward pigeons at each place saw the loft in the spot where it had been before, they flew to it and went inside.

And so, as a result of these and other such efforts, I became convinced that it was hopeless to work out a mobile-loft ESP test in the heavily wooded landscape of central North Carolina. I then turned to Dr. L. C. Graue, professor of mathematics at Coe College in Iowa and an experienced pigeon fancier. (He had attended our 1955 orientation conference at Duke.) Would he be interested, I asked, to see if he could succeed in getting pigeons to home to a mobile loft in Iowa? He gladly accepted the challenge.

Two summers of working with a pigeon loft made from an old milk delivery truck brought only frustrations. Even in the fairly open countryside around Cedar Rapids the pigeons sooner or later rebelled against staying with the loft, in spite of the fact that the birds were never set free more than half a mile away. It was not a question of whether they could find the loft. In many instances, they flew back to where it was and then, changing their minds about entering it, turned and flew out of sight. It seemed to be the same old story all over again: the loft did not stay put in one spot long enough to enable the birds to gain the necessary degree of familiarity with the environment to make them feel at home.

We made one further effort to overcome the distracting effect of landmarks. We moved the truck from Iowa to Plainview, Texas. This city is in a region that is as flat and as free of trees as anyone is likely to find anywhere. The loft was put in the hands of a student caretaker, and in October 1959, I went to Plainview to work with the pigeons.

The experimental plan was simple but effective for the question at issue. First, I separated the birds in the loft into two groups, experimentals and controls. For the control group, the truck was taken repeatedly to a particular spot on the plain and the birds were let out to fly just as if that was the location of an ordinary pigeon loft. The birds were unaccustomed to freedom when I first arrived, and a few members of the control group became confused or frightened and flew away before things settled down. In the end, however, the three pigeons left in that group appeared to feel at home at that particular spot as much as pigeons seem to feel at home around the usual stationary loft. (When the loft was parked at an assigned spot on the campus of Wayland College; when the loft was moving about; and when the experimental birds were flying, the control pigeons were closed in so that they could not see anything outside. Thus the landmarks around the selected control point were the only ones which the birds of that group came to know.)

The birds of the experimental group, on the other hand, were always allowed out of the loft for each exercise flight at an open spot on the plain where they had not been before. To the human observer, it was not easy to tell one spot from another. For the pigeons, however, apparently there *were* real differences. One by one the pigeons of the experimental group refused to return to the loft. They simply flew off, presumably to seek a new life under conditions that were stabler and more consistent with their nature.

That, in general terms, is the story, still not finished, of the efforts to find a crucial ESP test of pigeon homing. Such a test obviously requires that we find some way of forcing the issue in terms of the pigeon's homing behavior. It will never be sufficient simply to take the pigeon away from home and release it in the traditional manner. We are living in an age of science and technology when a submarine can make a journey under the arctic ice to the North Pole and return home without the members of the crew once having any doubt about where they have been. Similarly, who can say that a pigeon will be lost if we merely pick it up at night and haul it away in a lightproof box to a distance of one or two hundred miles? No, we must find some way that rules out even the remote possibility that the homing flight represents only the return half of a journey, both phases of which—the enforced outward part as well as the homeward flight—are recorded by some kind of in-nate inertial-guidance system analogous to that used in the submarine.

Is there yet some prospect that an ESP test of homing based on the principle of moving the loft instead of the pigeon can be found? Yes, there is, if someone can find or can create the opportunity to try it. The last best hope of a solution may lie in a suggestion that Dr. Kramer made on his very first visit, when he foresaw the possibility that landmarks might foil the efforts to work out the mobile-loft ESP test on land. Ultimately, he said, we might have to establish a pigeon loft aboard a ship or on a floating platform. The craft should, at least for the first few months, be anchored at one spot.

There would, of course, be some preparatory stages of the experiment. Only if these were passed successfully could the crucial stage be reached. It would be necessary to find out, for example, whether pigeons will thrive in a loft kept on the open sea.

Secondly, it would be necessary to see if they could establish for themselves a normal pattern of life, flying freely about the loft during the daytime and making themselves at home both in the superstructure and on the deck of the ship as well as in flights over the water. At present, for example, it is not even possible to assert that such pigeons would survive, since they might slowly perish from seasickness. But assuming that all went well, after four or five months we would have mature seaborne pigeons that had never seen a landmark.

Then it would be necessary to find out whether pigeons would home to the shipboard loft in its original location in the same manner as pigeons are now known to home to a stationary loft on land. This stage would also serve as a period of testing out various methods of releasing pigeons over the water to find which one served the best (submarine? plane? strange ship? smaller boat?) and what methods of tracking the birds would be most effective (pigeon-sized radio transmitter? use of suitable reflecting "window" for radar tracking? following by airplane or helicopter?). Let us assume that these tests are all successfully met and passed with flying pigeons.

Then we would be at a point at which we could begin to test whether pigeons are homing by ESP. For this purpose, visualize an equilateral triangle with 200-mile sides on the surface of the ocean, one point of which, A, is where the ship has been all the while. Another point, B, is a spot to which the pigeons will be taken to be released. The third point, C, is a position to which the ship will move while the pigeons are being taken to the release point.

Now the pigeons are released at B one at a time and the path of flight of each one is charted by the method found to be most suitable. The question is: Does the pigeon return to the now empty spot on the ocean, A, where it has spent its active life up till this time? Or does it go to the new spot, C, where the familiar loft *plus* the only visual environment the bird knows—the ship itself—are located? If the answer is A, the indications would be very strong indeed that there is some yet-to-be-discovered physical basis which forms a link for the pigeon between the release point B and the particular spot A on the surface of the globe. On the other hand, if the answer is C, the indications would be strong that the pigeon is homing on a basis which at least strongly suggests ESP.

In other words, the latter outcome of the experiment would logically be predicted if pigeon homing depends upon ESP, and it would not be predicted on the basis of any sensory hypothesis that has yet been offered. All physical explanations of homing assume that there is some sort of connecting link between the familiar home territory and the pigeon at the release point. Whatever this physical link might be, for all sensory hypotheses it is somehow assumed to be inseparably associated with the home loft as a *location* having a precise latitude-longitude position on the earth, and not as a target that can be moved simply by having the ship on which the loft is situated go sailing off to another spot on the ocean.

The general method of field studies the investigators have applied in the research described in this chapter is one that takes much time and great patience. Is the cost in effort too great to be justified by the prospects for a significant advance in knowledge? Measured in terms of the practical world of affairs, perhaps yes. And for most workers in the world of research, there are other things that are better for them personally to do. But from the point of view of science as such, there is no production schedule or established level of costs for new discoveries. In pure research, a problem is a problem is a problem, and it must be pursued to the end whether it takes five years or five hundred. The lifeblood of science is the men of patience and vision who ask nothing better than to be given the tools to do the jobs there are to be done. So the research on the problem of distance orientation in birds must and will go on, and the day will finally arrive when mankind will reap the benefit of a remarkable advance in knowledge that has been achieved by those who have fought the battle against ignorance on this particular sector of the long frontier of science.

This chapter illustrates also the fact that, while there are great men in science, the loss of a leader must not be allowed to put a stop to research. As the foregoing story has unfolded, I hope it has been clear who was the real hero. He was, of course, Dr. Gustav Kramer. In April 1958, Dr. Schmidt-Koenig interrupted a conference between Dr. Rhine and myself in the Parapsychology Laboratory to give us the sad news he had received from Wilhelmshaven: Dr. Kramer had suffered a fatal fall in Italy while climbing on the face of a cliff looking for wild rock pigeons to add to his experimental lofts. In his tragic death, bird orientation research suffered an irreparable loss, but those who had marched side by side with him have closed ranks and gone on with the work. This is, I feel sure, what he would have chosen as a memorial.

10

The Revolution Spreads

The aim of a revolutionary development in thought is to extend its influence. Axiomatically, the main concern of those who are committed to existing modes of thought is to resist the threat to their ways of thinking. A struggle inevitably ensues—a fight to the death of one or the other of the two contending ways of thinking. Nor dare we assume that just because a new idea deserves the label of Truth it will be welcomed upon its first application for admission to the fraternity of science. Can we yet say with assurance that parapsychology will succeed in winning acceptance on this try?

Any revolutionist worth his salt must, it goes without saying, believe in his cause and in its ultimate success. If this book has in any degree served its purpose, it should at least have engendered the feeling that the author is deeply involved as a parapsychologist. But the foregoing series of close-ups of developments in the field, described by one who has participated in or witnessed many of these events, may not by itself form a finished, unified picture of the movement. I feel an obligation, therefore, to attempt in a few final pages to tie together the threads of thought that the preceding chapters have in common.

Parapsychology is here to stay. This is not to say that its job is finished. Indeed, it has only been well started! But the time of testing by ordeal in the fire of scientific scorn has passed. No longer need a research worker fear the kind of scathing denunciation that Sir William Crookes and Sir William Barrett encountered when they ventured to present papers on their psi investigations to meetings of British scientists a few years before the Society for Psychical Research was founded. I am not implying that papers on parapsychology are received with rejoicing by those in charge of the programs of scientific conventions or by the editors of the psychological journals. But there is today a momentum, a forward thrust to psi research. This may be seen in the developments within the field as well as in the reactions to psi by those outside of parapsychology. Especially is it apparent from the way the field has put down new roots in different parts of the world. Some of these developments have been surprising even to the research workers.

A full account of the spread of the research and of the status that parapsychology has attained today as a world-wide branch of science is reserved (as I have said elsewhere) for a later book. But some hints regarding the magnitude of the developments that have already occurred and are still taking place may properly be revealed here.

Only within the past three years have scientists working in parapsychology in the West become aware of a parallel growth of research interest and activity in Russia. Since this significant fact first came to our attention we have made considerable progress in establishing close and cordial scientific relations with the Soviet scientists concerned. These relationships have been fostered by correspondence, by translation of relevant Russian publications, and by visits of parapsychologists to Russia to consult with the U.S.S.R. scientists who are taking the lead in this bold venture. In June 1962, I went as a representative of the Parapsychology Laboratory of Duke University to visit the newly established, state-supported laboratory for research on ESP at the University of Leningrad. I also talked with scientists in Moscow who are no less actively interested in the field though they were at that time less well organized.

These Russian parapsychologists are waging a successful campaign to gain the support of their fellow scientists and the educated public in Russia for research in this new area. As evidence of their success, we may note that three popular books on the subject by Soviet scientists have appeared recently. Two of these have been by Professor L. L. Vasiliev of Leningrad University, and his more recent one, published in 1962, had a first printing of 120,000 copies. It is said that when the Russians go in for any new interest in science or technology they do it with single-minded thoroughness. From the facts as they have been gradually emerging, it seems that their approach to parapsychology is going to be typical of their efforts in science.

Outside of the developments in Russia, new psi research centers are springing up at other places around the world. Some of these have already become productive, others are in an early or even formative stage. Altogether, however, they represent such a great research potential that even the *fact of their existence* makes exciting scientific news. Certainly the significance of these new developments is not escaping the psi research workers in the older centers. For example, by the fall of 1962 the Duke laboratory felt that its active relationship with the research in various places would benefit from the kind of attention that it is possible to give only after firsthand observation and exchanges of views. Accordingly, the laboratory asked me to go on a second trip. This one covered two months, from December 8, 1962, through February 8, 1963, and it took me westward across the U.S.A. and then on around the world to visit research centers in Japan, India, and Czechoslovakia.

So widespread is this new growth of interest in parapsychology that even the journey across the United States involved public lecturing and consulting with research workers in Texas and California, two states crossed on the journey in which newly organized efforts to initiate long-range programs of research in parapsychology are now taking shape.

The situation in Japan may properly be characterized as one of great promise. The most significant development there has been the establishment of the Institute for Religious Psychology under the direction of Dr. Hiroshi Motoyama. The objectives of this institute are concerned with the promotion of research on problems that are of concern to both psychology and religion, and Dr. Motoyama envisions parapsychology as comprising an important half of their program. (There can be no doubt of the historically close connection between spontaneous psi occurrences and the development of the great systems of religious thought.) One might illustrate the present prospects for parapsychology in Japan by commenting that what I learned there about the interest in this field would, by itself, have made my trip worth while.

The situation in India, however, presents an equally great challenge for parapsychology and also holds promise of major developments in the field over the next few years. In fact, so rapidly are things advancing in our field in India that the Duke laboratory sent a second representative, Dr. K. Ramakrishna Rao, to meet me there. Our joint mission was to discuss plans for a new parapsychological research center proposed by the University Grants Commission, the agency of the Union Government having general responsibility for the universities throughout that country. After our talks with the commission in New Delhi, Dr. Rao and I went our separate ways for two weeks. He visited universities throughout India to discuss the new center and to find the best location for it. I, in turn, worked in two of the states of northern India where ESP research projects were already under way with the support of the state governments. Everywhere we found enthusiastic interest in parapsychology and unreserved recognition that this is a branch of science for which India, because of her historical background of religious and philosophical thought and by virtue of her culture, should be eminently suited.

Since Dr. Rao and I returned to Duke, the plan which we submitted at the end of our visit has been officially approved by the University Grants Commission. The location for the new parapsychological research center will be Andhra University. Dr. Rao, even before our visit, had been selected as the director. He is now picking the Indian scientists who will comprise the permanent staff of the center and making plans to bring some of them to Duke for training.

The third place I visited abroad on this last trip was Prague, Czechoslovakia. Actually this was a second visit to Prague; my trip to Russia the preceding summer had included a five-day stay in that city. The purpose both times was to collaborate with Dr. Milan Ryzl, a young scientist who is doing ESP experiments there with an outstanding subject, Mr. Pavel Stepanek.

The distinctive thing about Dr. Ryzl's work is that he has apparently discovered a way to develop a subject's ability for good ESP test performance by a special method of training through hypnosis. Some questions remain to be answered by further research before it will be possible to state with the finality of a scientific conclusion just what the secret of Dr. Ryzl's success is. The combination of highly significant results obtained in his own experiments plus confirmation of this success in the joint work done with visiting scientists makes his contribution a unique one in parapsychology. In addition to our collaboration, three Dutch scientists on a more recent visit carried through a highly successful experiment with Mr. Stepanek. It is not surprising that, in the judgment of an increasing number of workers in the field, Prague is the most productive ESP research spot in the world at the present moment.

Every psychological struggle—and the psi revolution certainly can be so characterized—is a situation involving give and take. In this book we have naturally been concerned primarily with the giving: the efforts of a relatively few people to present the challenge of the field and its findings. What about the taking of what has been offered? How have the scientists and the educated, thinking non-scientists who have not been actively engaged in parapsychology reacted to what the psi research workers have been presenting to them? What has happened over the years to show that the parapsychologists are not simply wasting their efforts?

To the psi research workers themselves, the most highly prized signs of progress are those that show that other scientists are taking up the problems. These indications we have already touched upon in pointing out the spread of active interest and the emergence of new research centers around the world. These give the very best kind of assurance to the psi revolutionist that his labors are bearing fruit.

But not everyone who notices and reacts to the goings on in parapsychology can become an active participant in the research. Some, indeed, have been stirred to exert themselves in the opposite direction and have become outspokenly and aggressively critical. How have the critics of psi research made out in their efforts to discredit the subject?

Henry Sidgwick, in the first presidential address to

the Society for Psychical Research in 1882, predicted that the critics would stop at nothing to upset the findings of the parapsychologists. He said that therefore the investigators should strive to make their experimental safeguards so strong that the critic would be compelled to attack the good faith of the research workers themselves. This would be, in effect, a sign that the investigators had achieved the highest possible experimental standards.

Developments have proved that Professor Sidgwick was a sagacious prognosticator! It was many years before the critics gave up on the experimental procedures and mathematical methods. There were scattered criticisms during the first fifty years of experimental efforts. But when the evidence began to come in a great wave in the thirties in a way that threatened to take by storm the scientific bastion of the university laboratory itself, there was a corresponding increase in the ferocity of the critical attack.

Charges were first brought against the statistical methods, but these were soon cleared of the accusation of containing major flaws. The use of the balanced, "five-times-five" ESP pack gave results that did not fit precisely into the formulas that were applied, but these discrepancies were shown to be only minor errors of no practical consequence.

Then the critics tore into what they supposed were flaws in the experimental procedures: faulty shuffling and cutting of the cards; carelessness in guarding against sensory cues; errors in the recording and checking of the data; mistakes in checking the hits or in making the calculations; and so on and so on. This was the period when the experimenters knew that they were in a fight for their scientific lives. Therefore we answered each critical article as soon as it appeared. In view of the number of attacks and the consequent number of replies, it is no wonder that the decade of the thirties became known as the period of "The ESP Controversy." It came to an end with the symposium that the American Psychological Association organized for its annual meeting in Columbus, Ohio, in 1938. The book, *Extrasensory Perception After Sixty Years*, published in 1940 by five members of the Duke Parapsychology Laboratory research staff, was a fitting epitaph for the critics of that time. The ultimate critics whom Sidgwick foresaw had not yet appeared on the scene.

Before we give them their cue to come on stage for a brief re-enactment of their part in the drama, let me mention one Johnny-come-lately critic of the older style. This is Dr. B. F. Skinner, who waited ten years before breaking the pact of silence by which the psychologists attempted to quarantine the parapsychologists after 1938.

In the spring number of the 1948 *American Scientist*, Dr. Evelyn Hutchinson of Yale University devoted his regular feature column, "Marginalia," to a discussion of the ESP experiments which Dr. Soal and Mrs. Goldney had done with their outstanding subject, Mr. Basil Shackleton. Dr. Hutchinson chided the scientists, especially the psychologists, for their neglect of the evidence for ESP and challenged them to point out what was wrong with the experiments. In the summer issue of the periodical the editor turned the correspondence column over to Dr. Hutchinson to report the sequel to his challenge. He published one critical letter from a Harvard psychologist, Dr. Skinner, and a reply from Dr. Soal which gave him a reputation among the readers of the *American Scientist* as "the man who skinned Skinner." Even though Dr. Skinner's letter was selected as the most worthy of the criticisms received, it was apparent that what he wrote in his attack did not have even a kissin'-cousin relationship to what Dr. Soal and Mrs. Goldney had actually done in their experiments. For example, Dr. Skinner criticized Dr. Soal for depending upon cards shuffled by hand for his random order of target events. Dr. Soal replied that in his experiments cards were not used and no shuffling of any kind was involved.

If his was the best of the criticisms, one can only guess at the level of irrelevance of the others. Dr. Hutchinson's closing remarks are silent on this point, but they do speak eloquently regarding critics of parapsychology in general, as follows:

> The communication received from Professor Skinner was the only one casting doubt on the Soal and Goldney experiments that deserved any serious attention. Some other communications were received which give the impression that scientific opinion in this country is about equally divided on the validity of parapsychological research in general. It has also become very clear that the wishful thinking, which is often attributed to the proponents of this research, is equally attributable to the antagonists. Some

critical articles, published in reputable journals, to which my attention has been drawn, seem to me to transgress limits of fairness and good taste. If the parapsychologists are rightly required by their critics to maintain the highest possible standards of objectivity, it is only proper that their critics maintain an equal degree of objectivity, and that, in particular, they at least pay the parapsychologists the compliment of studying the original literature before criticizing it.

The next voice to be raised in opposition was heard in 1955, seven years later. (Now, at last, we encounter the sort of critic whom Sidgwick foresaw.) This was the attack on parapsychology by Dr. George R. Price, then of the University of Minnesota Medical School, the first critic openly to look for an escape from the findings in the suggestion that the parapsychologists themselves might have been grossly incompetent or that they could even consciously have resorted to trickery. Dr. Price, in his attack upon parapsychology in *Science*, in August 1955, showed that he had studied the evidence and had a profound respect for it. In fact, he started his critical article by admitting that he had been won over by the findings. But he had reconsidered his earlier conversion, and his article is mainly an explanation of how he could justify his rejection of the parapsychological evidence.

Dr. Price said that the results of parapsychology, chiefly those dealing with extrasensory perception, cannot be reconciled with the current scientific concepts of mechanism and materialism. He had come to see, therefore, that the conclusions of the parapsychologists must be accepted only if there is no alternative explanation. Since the better experiments as described make it impossible to reject the results on the basis of the usual kind of criticism, he points out that it is still conceivable that the scientists and academic people who took part in these key experiments could have participated in a deliberate fraud. ". . . it should be clearly understood that I am not here stating that Soal or any of his associates was guilty of deliberate fraud. All that I want to do is show that fraud was easily possible."

Thus the readers of *Science* were shown how they might escape from having to accept a universe in which ESP and similar phenomena are among the facts of nature. If this required making the assumption that scientists in many parts of the world, some of them with established reputations for scholarly work or research in other fields, might have connived to play parlor games with the purpose of fooling the human race into an acceptance of telepathy and clairvoyance, why hesitate to do so when the matter at issue is so great? Dr. Price appears to think that any alternative, even if it meant making scientific pariahs of the parapsychologists, is preferable to surrendering the cherished beliefs in a totally mechanistic, materialistic universe!

I do not intend in what I say here to be either adding to or taking away from the tone or import of Dr. Price's argument. If the position seems to be an extreme one, that is, I think, the position he chose. Consider, for example, how easily any finding in science that is not to one's liking could be brushed aside on the same basis. The point is that issues in science cannot be settled by raising a question of the lack of good faith on the part of the investigators. They must be settled, instead, by the patient, oftentimes plodding efforts of research and more research. And the directions the research takes must grow out of the phenomena Nature provides under her own conditions or they must come from the findings of earlier experiments. We cannot be guided by some arbitrary conception of what the effects claimed should be like and how we should be able to bring them to crucial test.

In his article, for example, Dr. Price proposed an experiment for the parapsychologists to perform as a crucial, do-or-die test of ESP. Perhaps such "command" performances will one day be possible—let us hope they will—but there is nothing to be gained by attempting to dictate our terms to Nature. As scientists, we have joined *her* game, and it is up to us to induce her to reveal the rules by which the game is played.

Another critic who showed that he would go to extremes in his efforts to remove the threat of psi from the scientific scene was Mr. C. E. M. Hansel of Manchester University in England. He indicated to Dr. Rhine in correspondence that he was a serious student of the research who would especially like an opportunity to study the evidence for clairvoyance. In so doing, he made no mention of the fact that he had already written a critical book, then in manuscript form, on the subject.

His correspondence with Dr. Rhine brought him the offer of expense money for a visit to the Parapsychology Laboratory, and this enabled him later to launch critical attacks on two of the earlier experiments. One was the

Pearce-Pratt Series, and the other an investigation known as the Pratt-Woodruff Series. Mr. Hansel's articles were published in the June 1961 number of the *Journal of Parapsychology*, and the answers that were published in the same issue appear to have satisfied even the critic himself, if his silence during the two years since that time may be taken as any indication. Rumor has it that he is still seeking to publish his book, but he was already more than twenty years behind the times in his previous criticism since he failed to take into account the crucial evidence for psi that has been published since 1939. He will never, at this rate, overtake the advancing research frontier!

But let us get off these trails through the sloughs of unsound and unsavory criticism and back onto higher ground. Over the years there have been those refreshing instants when the research workers in parapsychology have learned that the findings have won the favorable attention of some leader of scientific or intellectual thought. A few of these times mentioned by way of illustration must suffice here.

After the mid-century point, Dr. Julian Huxley was asked in England to nominate his choices for the great discoveries of the first half of the twentieth century. Among those he mentioned was the establishment of ESP.

The favorable attention of such men as Professor P. A. Sorokin of Harvard and Professor E. P. Sinnott of Yale testifies to the willingness of eminent scientists in other areas to entertain the findings and acknowledge their claim to serious consideration even though these scholars are not themselves drawn into an active participation in parapsychology.

Similarly, scientific groups have increasingly in recent years taken the initiative in planning meetings for the purpose of hearing *positive* presentations of parapsychology (unlike those earlier occasions that were designed to be purely *destructive*). These occasions at least betoken a readiness to listen and learn.

One particularly noteworthy instance of public attention to parapsychology happened without deliberate planning. Dartmouth College held a symposium in 1961 on the general topic of the mind-body relationship. The last meeting was a panel discussion in which one of the participants was Dr. Warren Weaver, vice-president of the Sloan Foundation. Dr. Weaver sat in silence until near the end of the program, when he spoke up to say that it had been a matter of some amazement to him that a symposium on the mind-body problem could have gone on for so long without anyone once mentioning the topic of ESP. He thought that this was a revealing commentary upon the state of American science. Whatever each one might personally think of the evidence for ESP, it was not justifiable simply to ignore it. Therefore he proposed that Dartmouth College should devote its next symposium to parapsychology. Those who witnessed the occasion said that the chairman was banging his gavel and calling for adjournment while President Dickey of Dartmouth was nodding his head in approval!

Many more names and incidents could be added to lengthen this list. These are enough, however, to show that parapsychology has at least created a slight intellectual ferment in the minds of some scientists. At the same time it is obvious that the spread of the psi revolution has not been a wind which has engulfed everyone in its path. Its advance is more selective: some people are affected while others seem immune.

In all modesty, I share the opinion that I heard my friend Milan Ryzl express: from now on, the progress of parapsychology cannot be stopped if man and his civilization survive. He was thinking of the scientific findings; but I would add that, even aside from these, the critics' self-appointed task of trying to obliterate the serious public interest in psi was hopeless from the start. This is due to the fact that *millions of people know on the basis of their own psi experiences* that there is something to it. Judge for yourself in case you are among this select number: Can you be told that something is superstitious nonsense when you already know that it is a basic facet of your own world of experience? You are only one member of a minority, but in total numbers you make up a multitude of people! You comprise the unshakable supporters of the psi revolution—those more fortunate ones who know at first hand what parapsychology is all about.

But the investigation of psi phenomena is not merely a holding action. Instead, it is very urgent business: we are engaged in a race for control over these unusual powers of the mind. It is not a race between Russia and the West to see which will be first with the great discovery about man's unique nature. This may develop in time, but what I have in mind is not a contest between two political camps. Rather, the race in parapsychology is a race of scientists against time. It is a race to extend scientific knowledge and understanding in a frontier zone regarding which man has been all too obviously and woefully ignorant until now. This is the frontier of human nature itself, of the meaning and nature of personality.

The race is concerned with discovering, on the sure basis of objective, experimental science, man's real place in the universe. The fact that there is a dangerous gap in scientific knowledge regarding the essential nature of man himself has been apparent for many years. My own inspired and inspiring teacher in psychology, Professor William McDougall, wrote in eloquent terms regarding the existence of this gap during the first third of this century. Even then he saw the imbalance between our highly advanced scientific knowledge of the physical world (giving us our dangerous technology of armaments and instruments of destruction) and our lack of knowledge regarding some of the most fundamental questions about mind as the root cause of the threat of annihilation that mankind faced between the two world wars.

The danger then was mild compared with the threat that hangs over all of us today! Confronted as we are with such unprecedented peril growing out of the triumphs of the physical sciences, we cannot escape by going back to the relative safety of an earlier era. The remedy needed is not less science but more. Man desperately needs an advance of knowledge which will bring him a real understanding of his own nature. For can we imagine that men who adequately understood them-

selves would be in constant danger of blasting one another from the face of the earth or that they would long
preserve the instruments for doing the job?

McDougall also most clearly recognized that what
was required for closing this gap in scientific knowledge
was a fresh approach. Even in his day he saw the research into psi phenomena as the means of lifting the
load of prejudice which has, during the last few centuries, so fully occupied the minds of the scientists. This
has led them to think in terms of the conception of
materialism which sees man as being essentially a freak-
ish combination of atoms.

The message of this book is that parapsychology
represents a new starting point in man's long and unending struggle to wrest from nature a fuller knowledge
of our universe. This start is different from earlier ones
in the simple but significant fact that the focus of scientific attention is upon *mind* instead of *matter*. What,
if anything, about man makes him unique? This question which has for so long been of concern to philosophers and religious thinkers as well as to poets and
other writers has at last, in parapsychology, begun to receive attention from scientists. The importance of this
new branch of inquiry needs to be recognized and appreciated not only by scientists but also by all intelligent, educated people.

Even though time is at a premium, gaining the widespread acceptance that the field needs and deserves will
not be easy. The difficulty is not one that is peculiar to
this research. It is always true of any really new and
revolutionary development in science that recognition

and acceptance come slowly. This is easy to understand. The pioneer scientist has hold of certain limited phenomena. He is impelled to pursue his observations of them only because he has an unshakable conviction of the importance of doing so. But for a long time he is not able to give an adequate picture of what his findings *mean*.

I could illustrate this difficulty by reference to any number of developments from the pages of the history of science. Imagine, for example, what Benjamin Franklin might have said if his contemporaries had asked him—as Franklin complained in fact they were doing! —what all the playing around with electrical sparks and flying kites into thunderclouds would ever amount to. Could we expect Franklin to describe a modern satellite hurtling through space millions of miles past the planet Venus and sending back electrical messages to tell us for the first time about actual conditions there? Or could anyone reasonably expect that Galileo, when he was begging his scientific colleagues merely to take a look through his telescope at the moons around the planet Jupiter, should have been able to persuade them by describing the universe known to modern astronomy as it extends for billions of light-years? The pioneer scientist is faced with an almost impossible task. This is to make sense out of what is necessarily still nonsense. Yet this is the task which must be faced if a new scientific venture is to succeed.

This book has tried to convey, as far as possible, a sense of the importance of parapsychology even at this early stage in its development. Its importance *at this juncture in history* is such that the spread of knowledge about the field cannot be put off until a later stage when it would undoubtedly be easier to understand its significance. When the very existence of mankind is staked on an "eyeball-to-eyeball confrontation" between our President and Khrushchev and the outcome (as someone so aptly said) may depend upon which is the first to blink, then not only the whole human race but even life itself as it exists on this planet is in a desperate race for survival.

ESP and the other simple, elusive phenomena studied by parapsychologists are to the further advance of scientific knowledge regarding human nature as Franklin's sparks were to the advance of knowledge in the area of electrical science and as Galileo's moons around Jupiter were to the advance of knowledge in the field of astronomy. These psi phenomena, defying as they do explanation in terms of purely mechanistic and physical principles, represent the exception to the prevailing scientific conceptions of man.

In science the exception *disproves* the rule. That is to say, scientific concepts cannot tolerate any exceptions. A fact which stubbornly refuses to be fitted into present theories must ultimately transform those theories. The facts of parapsychology have for more than eighty years refused to conform to conceptions of man that have led to the de-emphasizing, if not the outright denial, of the role of mind. Psi phenomena thus hold the promise of a revolutionary advance in man's understanding of himself. This is the psi revolution now in the making.

Suggested Further Reading

Heywood, R. *Beyond the Reach of Sense*. New York: Dutton, 1961.

Murphy, G. *Challenge of Psychical Research*. New York: Harper, 1961.

Rhine, J. B. *The Reach of the Mind*. New York: Sloane, 1947.

Rhine, J. B., and Pratt, J. G. *Parapsychology, Frontier Science of the Mind*. Springfield, Ill.: Thomas, 1957.

Rhine, L. E. *Hidden Channels of the Mind*. New York: Sloane, 1961.

Soal, S. G., and Bateman, F. *Modern Experiments in Telepathy*. New Haven: Yale, 1954.

Tyrrell, G. N. M. *Science and Psychical Phenomena* (1938) and *Apparitions* (1953). Joint re-issue. New York: University Books, 1961.

von Frisch, K. *The Dancing Bees*. New York: Harcourt Brace, 1955.

Index